The Sustaina
Mindset Principles

MW00811727

As we increase our awareness of the planetary challenges and how they intersect with the discipline or profession we choose to focus on, we have put our attention on the external forces and impacts. What remains untouched however is the set of beliefs, values, assumptions, mental processes, and paradigms that we hold and share: our mindset. But how do we change a mindset?

This book is the first to introduce the 12 Principles for a Sustainability Mindset, presenting educators with a framework that makes it easy to include them into teaching plans and lessons of any discipline. Written in a very clear and practical way, the book provides examples, checklists, tips, and tools for professionals and educators. It transforms the development of a much-needed mindset for sustainability into an accessible, fun and intuitive task.

The book is written with educators from a variety of disciplines in mind, including but not limited to management educators, coaches, and trainers. No other book comes close to providing such a well-organized and solid way of starting to shift our mindsets in the direction of sustainability.

Isabel Rimanoczy, author of *Big Bang Being: Developing the Sustainability Mindset* and *Stop Teaching,* has thirty years' experience as a researcher, author, and educator. She is the Convener of the PRME Working Group on the Sustainability Mindset, an international cohort of academics from 135 universities on five continents promoting innovation and a sustainability mindset. Global Ambassador of AIM2Flourish and Fellow of the Schumacher Institute.

Principles for Responsible Management series

Since the inception of the UN-supported Principles for Responsible Management Education (PRME) in 2007, there has been increased debate over how to adapt management education to best meet the demands of the 21st-century business environment. While consensus has been reached by the majority of globally focused management education institutions that sustainability must be incorporated into management education curricula, the relevant question is no longer why management education should change, but how.

Volumes within the Routledge/PRME book series aim to cultivate and inspire actively engaged participants by offering practical examples and case studies to support the implementation of the Six Principles of Responsible Management Education. Books in the series aim to enable participants to transition from a global learning community to an action community.

Editors

Milenko Gudić
Carole Parkes
Patricia M. Flynn
Kemi Ogunyemi
Amy Verbos

Books in the series:

Struggles and Successes in the Pursuit of Sustainable Development

Edited by Tay Keong Tan, Milenko Gúdic, and Patricia M. Flynn

"If we reach a sustainable future, it will be because visionary teachers call a new generation of citizens and leaders to the journey. Educators will find in this book a sophisticated conceptual framework and pedagogic toolkit for awakening students to the urgent challenge of sustainability and sparking their engagement as agents of transition."

—Paul D. Raskin, President, Tellus Institute, author of *Journey to Earthland: The Great Transition to Planetary Civilization*

"Isabel Rimanoczy's *The Sustainability Mindset Principles*, is a well research and practical approach to developing sustainability mindsets. Her book captures the complexity of mindsets that help us make sense of our world. Sustainability will not happen without sustainable mindsets. Believers and non-believers alike should read this book."

—Paul Shrivastava, Ph.D., Chief Sustainability Officer, Director, Sustainability Institute, Professor of Management, The Pennsylvania State University

"This is an essential reading for anyone teaching sustainability. Isabel shares simple and powerful tools that you can immediately use to make the learning experience with your students truly transformative. Your students will love these activities. The impact they make is a shifted mindset that prepares students to serve as responsible business leaders for a better world!'"

—Dr. Ekaterina Ivanova, National Research University "Higher School of Economics" Moscow

"In the current world situation, especially after the pandemic caused by COVID-19, this book is not only timely but necessary. In order to make this world a better place to live and work in, and not to limit ourselves merely to not impoverishing it, we need a new mindset that can be applied to all disciplines and jobs. Dr. Rimanoczy offers us 12 Sustainability Principles, which are sufficiently broad and practical to generate this mindset and to share it with others. Thanks to her extensive experience teaching students and practitioners, she brings together theory and practice in an extraordinary fashion, providing us with a guide to effectively create a positive impact on society."

—Ignacio Ferrero, Dean, School of Economics & Business, Universidad de Navarra

"Dr. Rimanoczy's latest book is a very useful vehicle for shifting students' mindsets and engaging them in actions needed to heal this broken world. I think it fits well with tool-oriented courses and programs aimed at taking appropriate and useful actions...and it recognizes that if we start with the proper mindset, everything else is natural, much easier, and much more impactful. Her book offers a useful framework for looking at who we need to become and guides us on how to get there. Dr. Rimanoczy, who may well be the leading expert on the planet on how to develop a sustainability mindset, builds effectively on more than a decade of dedicated work on discovering and describing the kind of mindset we need to move forward into the 21st Century."

—James A.F. Stoner, Chairholder: James A.F. Stoner Chair in Global Sustainability, Gabelli School of Business, Fordham University. Co-author with Frank Werner of *Financial Managing for a Sustainable World*

"Rarely do educators shine equal light on the role of the 'internal' aspect of leading sustainability and other critical complex adaptive challenges. All change begins with self, and leaders – with or without formal authority – must first understand the impact and influence they have on people and the systems within which they work and live. This requires a good deal of reflection as well. Sustainability Mindset Principles is comprehensive in both the practical external aspects of this work as well, in very pragmatic language and examples. The author has created numerous opportunities for everyone to see themselves as part of the solution. And finally, the power of the questions we pose to ourselves and others are fundamental to beginning the process of personal transformation, and ultimately systems transformation. This is a gift to educators, and the planet."

—Darcy Winslow, President/Co-Founder
Academy for Systems Change

"Many of us started a journey trying to passionately make 'a difference in the world,' only to be left wondering after a while whether that is achievable. When we turn inwards and try to address: What purpose do I strive for and what makes me happy, we begin to find answers which go beyond oneself and are fundamentally linked to the well-being of the people who are important to us. In my view, trying to find the compass and to go on this path is the single most important step one can take, and it might even bring about big changes to the world. This book helps to shed a light how to go about it, and is an important expression of the author's passion and work."

—Jonas Haertle, Special Assistant to the
Executive Director, United Nations Institute
for Training and Research, (UNITAR)

"It is an absolute pleasure to read the new book by Isabel Rimanoczy that discusses leadership, education, and changing mindsets within the context of the natural and human environment that develop recursively. In a straight forward language with clear and up to date examples, Isabel provides the reader with a set of valuable tools to help educators develop leaders with mindsets for the sustainable future. My advice for educators, sustainability experts and practitioners is: Read it, re-read it, live it."

—Prof. Danica Purg, President of IEDC-Bled School of Management, President of CEEMAN, Acting Chair of the PRME Steering Committee

"I celebrate this new book by Isabel Rimanoczy, which underlines the Greek philosophy stating that important events take place in their *kayros:* the right timing. *The Sustainability Mindset Principles* couldn't be more timely: when it's urgent to change a mindset to set the foundation for a new era. Education is the central pillar of this transformation, and in this context, the contribution of Isabel Rimanoczy is not only valuable, but much needed."

—Silvia Zimmermann del Castillo, Author, President of the Argentine Chapter of the Club of Rome

"Deeply insightful and grounded in the histories of meaning making across cultures, this guide for educators brings issues of sustainability to personal relevance for all students. In an engaging series of reflections, it leads them to craft their own path to ensure the well-being of the planet and all its living systems."

—Mary Watson, Ph.D., Executive Dean, The New School

"Practical and thoughtful, Rimanoczy's book invites educators to deeply reflect how to develop the sustainable mindset needed—along with the knowledge and skills—to tackle the most pressing global issues and achieve the Sustainable Development Goals (SDGs) through a shift in 'knowing' (ecoliteracy), 'thinking' (systemic and innovative thinking) and 'being' (values, purpose). This is, indeed, highly needed."

—M. Florencia Librizzi, Head of Program and Partnerships, SDG Academy, UN Sustainable Development Solutions Network (SDSN)

"Rimanoczy writes about educating for and changing mindsets on global sustainability with the drive of an entrepreneur and the zeal of a missionary."

—Tay Keong Tan, PhD, Director of International Studies and Leadership Studies, Radford University

The Sustainability Mindset Principles

A Guide to Developing a Mindset for a Better World

Isabel Rimanoczy

Routledge
Taylor & Francis Group

LONDON AND NEW YORK

First published 2021
by Routledge
2 Park Square, Milton Park, Abingdon, Oxon OX14 4RN

and by Routledge
52 Vanderbilt Avenue, New York, NY 10017

Routledge is an imprint of the Taylor & Francis Group, an informa business

© 2021 Isabel Rimanoczy

The right of Isabel Rimanoczy to be identified as author of this work has been asserted by her in accordance with sections 77 and 78 of the Copyright, Designs and Patents Act 1988.

All rights reserved. No part of this book may be reprinted or reproduced or utilised in any form or by any electronic, mechanical, or other means, now known or hereafter invented, including photocopying and recording, or in any information storage or retrieval system, without permission in writing from the publishers.

Trademark notice: Product or corporate names may be trademarks or registered trademarks, and are used only for identification and explanation without intent to infringe.

British Library Cataloguing-in-Publication Data
A catalogue record for this book is available from the British Library

Library of Congress Cataloging-in-Publication Data
Names: Rimanoczy, Isabel, 1956- author.
Title: The sustainability mindset principles : a guide to develop a mindset for a better world / Isabel Rimanoczy.
Description: Abingdon, Oxon ; New York, NY : Routledge, 2021. | Series: The principles for responsible management education series | Includes bibliographical references and index. |

Identifiers: LCCN 2020020939 (print) | LCCN 2020020940 (ebook) | ISBN 9780367551797 (hardback) | ISBN 9780367559007 (paperback) | ISBN 9781003095637 (ebook)
Subjects: LCSH: Mindfulness (Psychology) | Sustainability. | Self-consciousness (Awareness)
Classification: LCC BF637.M56 R56 2021 (print) |
LCC BF637.M56 (ebook) | DDC 158.1--dc23
LC record available at https://lccn.loc.gov/2020020939
LC ebook record available at https://lccn.loc.gov/2020020940

ISBN: 978-0-367-55179-7 (hbk)
ISBN: 978-0-367-55900-7 (pbk)
ISBN: 978-1-003-09563-7 (ebk)

Typeset in Bembo
by KnowledgeWorks Global Ltd.

To the voices that came before me, waking us up. May your message be carried in the pages of this book, reaching minds, hearts, and hands ready to act.

Contents

Foreword

As awareness of social and global challenges expands, sustainability education is growing in popularity. This is the case across disciplines and institutions, including business education that, despite falling enrolments, continues to confer the most awarded undergraduate and graduate degrees in the United States. The Association to Advance Collegiate Schools of Business (AACSB), the world's largest and most widely recognized business accreditation body, and the one to which all reputable business schools pay homage, is revising its standards in 2020. The standards now require business schools to demonstrate a positive social impact. Standard 4.3 states that accredited schools must document curricular elements within formal coursework that "foster and support students' ability to have a positive impact on society." Positive social impact is defined as addressing broader social, economic, business, and/or physical environment issues through internal or external initiatives. In parallel, new rating systems are emerging to assess business schools based on their positive impact in the world. The Positive Impact Rating (PIR) announced at Davos in January 2020 is one such system.

Educating future business leaders who will have a positive impact on society is a noble goal. But how are business schools to do it? Educational strategies have ranged from "making the business case" for social and environmental

performance to discourses on ethics, regulatory policies, and new technologies such as Artificial Intelligence
and CRISPR, to teaching new metrics from the Global
Reporting Initiative (GRI) and the Sustainability
Accounting Standards Board (SASB). Despite these strategies, indicators of human progress on issues such as climate
change and income inequality continue to show worsening
trends. This is because sustainability is too often focused
on doing less harm, as with corporate goals to reduce carbon emissions or cut waste. Such actions help businesses be
less unsustainable. In other words, they reduce the amount
of harm done. *Such actions should never be confused with making a positive impact.*

By shining a bright light on the sustainability mindset, Isabel Rimanoczy offers an important new avenue for
business educators. Much has been written about changing mindset in business but few educators have, until
now, been given a roadmap for how to do it. In this book,
readers discover a useful framework and practical steps to
intervene in educational systems where it can make the
biggest difference.

Systems scientist Donella Meadows wrote that the
highest leverage point at which to intervene in a system
is in "the mindset or paradigm out of which the system
arises." About this highest leverage point, she said the
following.

> The shared idea in the minds of society, the great big
> unstated assumptions—unstated because unnecessary
> to state; everyone already knows them—constitute
> that society's paradigm or deepest set of beliefs about
> how the world works … [For example] growth is
> good. Nature is a stock of resources to be converted
> to human purposes. Evolution stopped with the emer-
> gence of *Homo sapiens*. One can "own" land. Those
> are just a few of the paradigmatic assumptions of our
> current culture, all of which have utterly dumfounded

other cultures, who thought them not the least bit obvious (Meadows, 1999: 18)

It is no less such a transformation that Dr. Rimanoczy proposes for educators: A powerful shift in individual and collective behaviors based on a revolution in the paradigmatic beliefs, values, assumptions, and social norms that we hold.

The choice facing business schools is to accept the MBA program for what it is, a functional training ground, or to see it as a leadership development opportunity. The institutional role of business in this context increasingly needs to help address social and global issues by creating prosperity for all while contributing to a healthy natural environment and improving human well-being. Without acknowledging such a transformation in the role of business, educators are blindly building—with no thought to relevance—on today's theories and practices that, at best, tangentially reduce social harm or ecological footprints and, at worst, explicitly contribute to growing social crises and environmental disaster.

Organized around 12 Sustainability Mindset Principles, Dr. Rimanoczy's years of experience with students and business leaders, amplified through her exchanges and dialogs with educators around the world, provides a trusted guide to transforming mindset. The approach blends scholarship and practice, research findings and inquiry, rational-empirical analysis with direct-intuitive skills. Each of the 12 Principles is made accessible for classroom use through key teaching goals, curricular components, tips & tricks, appreciative inquiry, and exercises. Such pedagogy is particularly effective when grounded in the educator's self-awareness, since the internal aspects of mindset are as important for the educator as they are for the students.

We already have the technical tools and knowledge to make sustainability take hold in business education. Steps are being taken in finance, agriculture, and energy, to name just a few domains in transition. From true cost accounting and regenerative agriculture to supply chains designed for a circular economy and financial market incentives for long-term value rather than fractional trading, the building blocks exist for a sustainable future. What is needed now is a concerted worldwide effort to seriously incorporate these ideas into business school curricula and research agendas, restoring such pedagogy and scholarship to powerful avenues for economic transformation toward a greater good. Dr. Rimanoczy's new volume is an important contribution to this end.

Chris Laszlo
March 2, 2020

Preface

As I am finishing up the manuscript, I realize that the world has dramatically changed in a very short time. COVID-19 is the tiny being that has infiltrated into our bodies, our economy, and borders of nations protected by walls, guards, or customs agents. It changed how we greet, how we work, how we entertain ourselves. It altered our daily activities in such a way that it made us revise priorities. It pulled us into our homes, connected us with family and friends in new ways. It shook off all the lines occupied in our calendars and made us figure out what to do with our newly available time. It developed empathy and social sensitivity, allowing us to experience a profound sense of interdependency and connection. So much so that we expanded our selfish and sometimes reduced circle of care to a wider circle—realizing that if we care for others we will all be better off.

This little COVID-19 bug has made us stop reckless consumption and focus on the essential needs. It has made us appreciative of the health workers and of the strangers posting humorous or artistic creations for the pleasure of others. It gave us back time, hours that we thought "had" to be allocated to "important things." As a very busy friend reflected: "I am not sure I will be able to go back to the life I had before…this is nice!"

Yes, it has brought pain and suffering and death and uncertainty. It has also brought back fish in the canals of Venice, clear skies in China, dolphins in the Adriatic Sea. It has forced upon us the need to make meaning, extract some wisdom, capture the larger message that is coming to us. COVID-19 has enabled all of us to advance three feet in our own developmental journey.

As I am writing this Preface, I wonder what the coming months will bring. We may flatten the curve, we may get over this sooner or perhaps later than imagined. New challenges will certainly be appearing along the way, as we are called to reset a lost balance with ourselves, each other, and all Nature. We may bounce back to "more usual patterns." But one thing is sure: We will never be the same. This experience will have contributed to our understanding and let some light in that we didn't imagine could be there. It gave us the first total, collective, global experience that a different way of living is actually possible.

How will we educators respond and adapt to this new consciousness? How are we going to keep the flame alive; how are we going to nurture the sparks of hope, imagination, and a new way of being in the world that works for all? How are we going to take this unexpected opportunity to enhance a new paradigm, foster a new connectedness, help grow the roots of this new way of thinking, acting, and being on this planet?

We cannot simply go back to teaching our courses as usual, as before. A tiny bug has come to connect us with the higher angels of our nature, and as I write this, everyone in their own way is having that experience. We cannot let this pass. In fact, this is our first task: How to hold on this moment of wisdom, bring it back, help us all ponder, reflect, and invent new possibilities of shaping a better life. The Principles presented in the following pages can provide some guidance for educators in how to draw out and share the vital lessons of this crisis.

About the author

What can I do with my skills to make a difference in the time I'm given on this planet? This is the question Isabel Rimanoczy asked herself, which led her to connect her passion for transformative learning with sustainability and make her goal to develop "change accelerators." In her research at Columbia University, she found the leverage points to develop a Sustainability Mindset and focused on creating materials, frameworks, and pedagogical approaches to awaken in every individual the spiritual, emotional, and cognitive resources to become an agent for shaping a better world. She sees the multiplying impact of developing educators: Each year every instructor has the opportunity to inspire and engage hundreds of students.

With a background in psychology and business administration, she worked over 20 years as a coach with individuals and corporate leadership teams from around the world. She brought that experience into the higher education sector, working with pioneering educators eager to act as holistic learning facilitators for a new paradigm.

In 2013, she created LEAP! (Leverage resources, Expand awareness, Accelerate change, and Partner), a global network of academics interested in developing a Sustainability Mindset. The network became part of PRME (Principles for Responsible Management Education), an initiative of the UN Global Compact, as the Working Group of the Sustainability Mindset, with members from 49 countries.

Isabel is a sought-after speaker at international conferences and events and has published over 140 papers and book chapters. She is the author of Big Bang Being: Developing the sustainability mindset (2013) and Stop Teaching (2016).

She is a senior partner in Leadership in Motion (LIM LLC and Director and co-founder of Minervas.org, Women changing the world, a 501 (c) (3) organization to develop women as conscious change agents through circles of art and dialog.

www.IsabelRimanoczy.net

Acknowledgments

The slow maturation of the 12 Sustainability Mindset Principles over the past years occurred in large part thanks to the courageous members of LEAP!, scholars from around the world who know they are outliers seeing beyond what we are used to seeing. Their stories inspired me, their questions challenged me, their perspectives intrigued me, and their passion continuously lights my fire. For the opportunity to publish this book, I am thankful to Rebecca Marsh, who listens and is always open to new ideas. The speed in converting my ideas into a proper manuscript has to be credited to a whole team: my Emeritus Editor, Tony Pearson, my dear colleague Kent Fairfield, and my friend Veronica Legrand, all of them carefully exploring what my sometimes unusual English expressions may want to say. Your editing magic made this book so much better. To Kent, Jeff Salzman, and Tom Culham, my gratitude for their comments and suggestions for a richer content. To Ekaterina Ivanova, Darcy Winslow, Amelia Naim Indrajaya, and Michael Lees, I thank you for your stories and exercises. To Karthyeni Sridaran, Jody (Louis) Fry, Jim Stoner, Alexander Nuer, and Margaret Goralski, my gratitude for your participation in the Atelier that nurtured and enriched my thinking of the Principles. To Tay Keong Tan, my gratitude for suggesting the creation of a repository of pedagogical materials on the Sustainability Mindset, organized around these 12 Principles. To Megan Buchler, thank you for checking accuracy and to Chris Laszlo for your generous Foreword. This Foreword came on the 7th anniversary of his dad's Foreword to my *Big Bang Being* book. What an honor the Laszlo family has bestowed on my writing. To Martine Marie, my thinking partner who makes work fun, my endless gratitude. To Clara Arrocain, for her question, "What will the next book be about?" when I'm barely finishing one manuscript. Your challenge is inspiring. To Jim Stoner, I am grateful for the continuous support throughout the years, and to Aixa Ritz, for starting all of this when you invited me to create a course on developing the Sustainability Mindset. To Jim, Sandra Waddock, Shelley Mitchell, and Christof Miska, my gratitude for the review of this proposal and your support on many occasions in making valuable suggestions and introductions. To Kerul Kassel, who in the early days suggested we needed a "model, a framework" and tirelessly led our meetings with Shelley to develop the Sustainability Mindset Model, presented in papers, journal, and chapter submissions. Everyone's role in promoting a new mindset is getting us closer to living in the world we want. To Chris Murray, my gratitude for accompanying me once again in this new project with professional rigor and time sensitivity, such a rare combination. To Sophie Peoples, for her caring attention to details and support to make this project a tangible book. To Ernie Turner, my life partner, who celebrates with me every day the joy of little things and who has the gift of dreaming big in easy ways. You make life a fun adventure and brought much wisdom to my life.

Fort Lauderdale,
April 30, 2020

Part I

Introduction

Some years ago I had this thought: Why are some leaders able to champion initiatives in their corporations that help reduce their environmental or social impact, or even better, make a positive impact? What is it that they know, what motivated them to step away from "business as usual" and take on "the road less traveled"? And what if it was something we could intentionally develop to influence the shaping of a new generation of leaders?

There are some thoughts that are powerful seeds. We don't know it at the moment, but in hindsight, we can recognize them as the starting point of something significant.

In this case, the thought led to my doctoral research, and six years later I had identified a number of elements that played a key role in the mindset shift of pioneering leaders—elements that actually could be developed. I called it the Sustainability Mindset. The elements related to the knowing (ecoliteracy), thinking (systemic and innovative thinking), and being (values, purpose) (Rimanoczy, 2010).

The next step followed naturally: By invitation of Prof. Aixa Ritz at Fairleigh Dickinson, I designed for the first time a course to develop those aspects. Converting the elements into learning objectives, it became clear that they fell into specific content areas: Ecological Worldview,

Systems Perspective, Emotional and Spiritual intelligence. And all this anchored in action: Projects to make a difference (Kassel, Rimanoczy, & Mitchell, 2016; Rimanoczy, 2014).

The first teaching experience brought its surprises: After a few weeks into the semester, the transformational insights of the students started to multiply. By the end of the 13 weeks, a clear shift in their mindset had taken place. They had changed the way they saw the world, but more importantly, how they saw themselves in it, their role, and purpose. They ended the course with passionate plans to make a difference through their profession, work, and community. The small project they had worked on gave them the confidence that while challenges were great, they had a role they could play, and it was worth it.

That experience repeated itself with every new group of students, in the same university and others. After five years, I thought that with 25 students at a time change would take long. I invited some colleagues to form a learning community of professors interested in developing a mindset for sustainability. The name LEAP! (Leverage resources, Expand awareness, Accelerate change, and Partner) was both a declaration of purpose and a vision: That we collectively could generate a leap forward, influencing the shaping of a better world.[1]

What happened since 2014 was indeed a *leap*. Scholars from around the world joined the network, as it resonated with something they were already concerned with, something that they were experimenting with in their own institutions, or something they felt was missing in their teaching. The diversity of contexts and geography— the Americas, Asia, Europe, Africa, and Asia Pacific— indicated that the call for a mindset shift was a widespread need. Through hundreds of hours of virtual exchanges and meetings, the members of the LEAP! network found inspiration for papers, articles, academic presentations, symposia, chapters, and whole books. They created and shared best practices, new frameworks, and context-specific developments, such as how to embed a sustainability mindset in the College of Tropical Agriculture in Ghana; in English writing classes in Hawaii; in classes of architecture and tourism management; and across management education courses (Kassel & Rimanoczy, 2018). From Finland to Argentina, from Sri Lanka to Maui, developing a Sustainability Mindset took as many shapes as the diversity of the professors: In mandatory or elective courses; for undergrads or graduates; embedded into a whole course or as a module; in the visionary creation of the Center for Sustainability Mindset and Corporate Responsibility in Jakarta; in the inspiration of the deans of the 160 business schools in Colombia; in TED talks by professors; or in corporate leadership programs. With ambassadors in Austria, Scotland, Germany, Russia, China, and the Philippines, the network continues to grow.

No one way

There is no one way to develop a mindset for sustainability. The proof is in the richness and variety these 155-plus professors have shown over the years in how they are experimenting, and in how they are achieving the goals. New research, from within and outside of this network, seeks ways to understand and develop a new mindset, focusing on: Addressing the economic paradigm (Pirson, 2017a; 2017b; Werner & Stoner, 2018), entrepreneurship and innovation (Indrajaya, 2018; Schaltegger, Lüdeke-Freund, & Hansen, 2016), environmental stewardship (Bennett et al., 2018), systems thinking (Capra, 2007), quantum physics (Tsao & Laszlo, 2019), humanistic approaches (Colbert, Nicholson, & Kurucz, 2018; Pirson, 2020), human development stages (Hochachka, 2019; O'Brien & Hochachka, 2010), positive psychology (Cooperrider & Fry, 2012), spirituality and spiritual leadership (Dhiman & Marques, 2016; Fry & Slocum, 2008; Zsolnai, 2015), transformative learning (Brunnquell & Brunstein, 2018; Brunnquell, Brunstein, Jaime, 2015; Sipos, Battisti, & Grimm, et al, 2008; Sterling, 2001, 2008), consciousness (Eaton, Hughes, & MacGregor, 2016; Tsao & Laszlo, 2019; Wamsler & Brink, 2018), aboriginal and ancestral wisdom (Burns, 2015; Wall & Masayesva, 2004), and religious scriptures (Leary, Minton, & Mittelstaedt, 2016; Minton, Kahle, & Kim, 2015). A few opt for Nature or art as a medium (Antonacopoulou & Taylor, 2018; Purg & Sutherland, 2017; Yang, Ivanova, & Hufnagel, 2019), or an encompassing holistic approach, such as the pedagogy used at the unique Schumacher College in Totnes, UK.

The explosion of the landscape into so many different approaches is just what we need, at a planetary level. In this context, what is the place of the Sustainability Mindset Principles?

As part of the grounded theory that is being created, I wanted to formulate some simple principles that would address each of the key elements for developing a Sustainability Mindset. The experience with students, amplified through the exchanges and dialogs with colleagues from around the world nurtured my thinking, confirming, modifying, and adding to the original research findings. The vision was to have a few principles, clear and easily understandable statements, which could guide educators around the world to find ways to embed sustainable mindset goals into their lesson plans.

The result is the set of 12 Sustainability Mindset Principles (SMP) introduced in this book. They are sufficiently general to be applied to any discipline, and sufficiently specific that they be a scaffolding for educators structuring learning goals. They touch transversally many of the existing scholarly approaches to a Sustainability Mindset mentioned above; the goal of the Principles is to be at the service of these approaches rather than replacing or questioning any of them. To the recurring question, "Yes, a mindset shift is urgent, but HOW can we do that?," the SMP hope to provide help in guiding readers to answer that question.

How is this book organized?

We start with an overview of the Sustainability Mindset, including its definition, and follow with the content areas of the Sustainability Mindset model.

Each Principle is then covered in a dedicated chapter. Each chapter introduces the Principle with its definition, its origin, and its scholarly foundation. The chapter then lists the key components and the teaching goals that represent the Principle. Next, it addresses implementation, including tips for educators to prepare themselves. Facilitating the development of a sustainability mindset requires some preparation from the educator. This preparation relates not only to materials and possible exercises, but actually starts with expanding self-awareness, since the internal aspects of the mindset will touch the educator as much as the students.

For this reason each principle will be presented with a section of Key Questions for the educator, inviting readers to pause, reflect, and perhaps use journaling to explore questions that may be new for them.

Each Principle presents an example of a tool or activity that can be inserted into a lesson plan, and a story, and concludes with some further resources and references.

The volume wraps up with a brief review of the pedagogical approach required for the development of a mindset and provides guides to educators to transition from a teaching-focused to a learning-focused methodology. Finally, we connect the dots and ponder what does this all mean? What is the impact of developing a new mindset? What is the better world we will be shaping?

Note

1. In 2015, the group became the PRME Working Group on the Sustainability Mindset.

References

Antonacopoulou, E. P. & Taylor, S. S. (Eds.). (2018). *Sensuous learning for practical judgment in professional practice: Volume 2: Arts-based interventions* (Vol. 2). Berlin, Germany: Springer.

Bennett, N. J., Whitty, T. S., Finkbeiner, E., Pittman, J., Bassett, H., Gelcich, S., & Allison, E. H. (2018). Environmental stewardship: A conceptual review and analytical framework. *Environmental Management*, *61*(4), 597–614.

Brunnquell, C. & Brunstein, J. (2018). Sustainability in management education: Contributions from critical reflection and transformative learning. *Metropolitan Universities*, *29*(3), 25–42.

Brunnquell, C., Brunstein, J., & Jaime, P. (2015). Education for sustainability, critical reflection and transformative learning: Professors' experiences in Brazilian administration courses. *International Journal of Innovation and Sustainable Development*, *9*(3–4), 321–342.

Burns, H. L. (2015). Transformative sustainability pedagogy: Learning from ecological systems and indigenous wisdom. *Journal of Transformative Education*, *13*(3), 259–276.

Capra, F. (2007). Sustainable living, ecological literacy, and the breath of life. *Canadian Journal of Environmental Education*, *12*(1), 9–18.

Colbert, B. A., Nicholson, J., & Kurucz, E. C. (2018). Humanistic leadership for sustainable transformation. In *Evolving leadership for collective wellbeing: Lessons for implementing the United Nations sustainable development goals* (pp. 33–47). London: Emerald Publishing Limited.

Cooperrider, D. L. & Fry, R. (2012). Mirror flourishing and the positive psychology of sustainability. *Journal of Corporate Citizenship*, *46*(1), 3–12.

Dhiman, S. & Marques, J. (2016). *Spirituality and sustainability*. New York, NY: Springer International Publishing.

Eaton, M., Hughes, H. J., & MacGregor, J. (Eds.). (2016). *Contemplative approaches to sustainability in higher education: Theory and practice*. London: Routledge.

Fry, L. W. & Slocum, J. W. (2008). Maximizing the triple bottom line through spiritual leadership. *Organizational Dynamics*, *37*(1), 86.

Hochachka, G. (2019). On matryoshkas and meaning-making: Understanding the plasticity of climate change. *Global Environmental Change*, *57*, 101917.

Indrajaya, A. N. (2018). Spiritual development programs, individual spirituality and sustainability mindset toward higher commitment to social and environmental impact. *International Journal of Business Studies*, 2(3), 150–163.

Kassel, K., Rimanoczy, I., & Mitchell, S. F. (2016). The sustainable mindset: Connecting being, thinking, and doing in management education. In *Academy of management proceedings* (Vol. 2016, No. 1, p. 16659). Briarcliff Manor, NY: Academy of Management.

Kassel, K. & Rimanoczy, I. (Eds.). (2018). *Developing a sustainability mindset in management education*. London: Routledge.

Leary, R. B., Minton, E. A., & Mittelstaedt, J. D. (2016). Thou shall not? The influence of religion on beliefs of stewardship and dominion, sustainable behaviors, and marketing systems. *Journal of Macromarketing*, *36*(4), 457–470.

Minton, E. A., Kahle, L. R., & Kim, C. H. (2015). Religion and motives for sustainable behaviors: A cross-cultural comparison and contrast. *Journal of Business Research*, *68*(9), 1937–1944.

O'Brien, K. & Hochachka, G. (2010). Integral adaptation to climate change. *Journal of Integral Theory and Practice*, *5*(1), 89–102.

Pirson, M. (2017a). Working Alternatives-From Capitalism to Humanistic Management? *Humanistic Management Association, Research Paper Series*, (17–25).

Pirson, M. (2017b). *Humanistic management: Protecting dignity and promoting well-being*. Cambridge, UK: Cambridge University Press.

Pirson, M. (2020). A humanistic narrative for responsible management learning: An ontological perspective. *Journal of Business Ethics*, *162*, 1–19.

Purg, D. & Sutherland, I. (2017). Why art in management education? Questioning meaning. *Academy of Management Review*, *42*, 382–396.

Rimanoczy, I. B. (2010). *Business leaders committing to and fostering sustainability initiatives*. New York, NY: Teachers College, Columbia University.

Rimanoczy, I. (2014). A matter of being: Developing sustainability-minded leaders. *Journal of Management for Global Sustainability*, *2*(1), 95–122.

Schaltegger, S., Lüdeke-Freund, F., & Hansen, E. G. (2016). Business models for sustainability: A co-evolutionary analysis of sustainable entrepreneurship, innovation, and transformation. *Organization & Environment*, *29*(3), 264–289.

Sipos, Y., Battisti, B., & Grimm, K. (2008). Achieving transformative sustainability learning: Engaging head, hands and heart. *International Journal of Sustainability in Higher Education, 9*(1), 68–86.

Sterling, S. (2001). *Sustainable education: Re-visioning learning and change. Schumacher briefings.* Cambridge, UK: Green Books for the Schumacher Society.

Sterling, S. (2008). Sustainable education – towards a deep learning response to unsustainability. *Policy & Practice – A Development Education Review,* 6(Spring), 63–68.

Tsao, F. C. & Laszlo, C. (2019). *Quantum leadership: New consciousness in business.* Palo Alto, CA: Stanford University Press.

Wall, D. & Masayesva, V. (2004). People of the corn: Teachings in Hopi traditional agriculture, spirituality, and sustainability. *American Indian Quarterly, 28,* 435–453.

Wamsler, C. & Brink, E. (2018). Mindsets for sustainability: Exploring the link between mindfulness and sustainable climate adaptation. *Ecological economics, 151,* 55–61.

Werner, F. M. & Stoner, J. A. (2018). Sustainability and the evolution of the shareholder wealth maximization paradigm. In *Research handbook of finance and sustainability* (p. 179). Cheltenham, UK: Edward Elgar Publishing.

Yang, C., Ivanova, E., & Hufnagel, J. (2019). Using contemplative photography in sustainability management education: Pedagogical applications in the United States, Russia, and Germany. Paper presented at the Academy of Management Specialized Conference "Responsible Leadership in Rising Economies", Bled, Slovenia.

Zsolnai, L. (2015). *The spiritual dimension of business ethics and sustainability management.* Berlin, Germany: Springer.

1 What is a Sustainability Mindset?

With the proliferation of sustainability courses and modules in higher education, it is clear that institutions are conscious of the urgency to focus on sustainability knowledge, facts, and data. In doing so, attention is predominantly concentrated on the "External" or visible aspects of sustainability.

These aspects, in turn, are observable at both an individual and a collective level. As Figure 1.1 shows, at the individual level, the focus is on developing skills, behaviors, competencies, entrepreneurial habits, and an understanding and increased knowledge of sustainability. At the collective level, the focus is on regulations, policies, innovations, benchmarks, best practices, agreements, Sustainable Development Goals (SDGs), new reporting frames, trends, etc.

Interestingly, improved access to information and knowledge alone doesn't seem to be reflected in a proportional increase in sustainability actions that tackle the global challenges.[1] Research is increasingly pointing out the need to address other aspects at the foundation of our habits and actions: Our paradigms, values, and worldviews—in essence, our mindset (Elgin, 2009; Kumar, 2002; Meadows, 1997; Smith & Sharicz, 2011; Speth, 2009; Tsao & Laszlo, 2019; Wamsler & Brink, 2018, p. 59).

These are internal, less visible, aspects that play a powerful role in influencing how people respond to the

External

Individual

Collective

Behaviors
Habits
Initiatives
Leadership

Regulations
Innovations
Solutions
Programs
Institutions...

Figure 1.1 External focus of sustainability education

challenges. The Sustainability Mindset belongs to the **Internal** column in both the individual and collective arena (Figure 1.2). At the internal-individual level, it is molded by a person's values, sense of purpose, preferences, assumptions, and beliefs. At the internal-collective level, the focus is on collectively shared values, beliefs, and narratives (paradigms).

This said, as the definition presented below shows, a Sustainability Mindset is in itself not visible, of course, but it is visible *in action*.

Definition

The Sustainability Mindset is defined as "a way of thinking and being that results from a broad understanding of the ecosystem's manifestations, from social sensitivity, as well as an introspective focus on one's personal values and higher self, and finds its expression in actions for the greater good of the whole" (Kassel, Rimanoczy, & Mitchell, 2018, p 7).

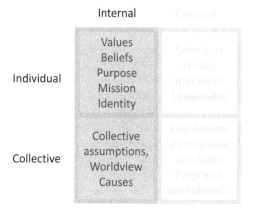

Figure 1.2 The focus of the Sustainability Mindset

Source: Adapted from AQAL, Wilber (2005).

Let's take a closer look at each component of this definition that lies at the foundation of the 12 Sustainability Mindset Principles, beginning with:

A way of thinking and being...

The first section of the definition refers to rational and cognitive thinking, the "thinking dimension," and to the ontological aspects, grouped in the "being dimension." There is a historical and cultural separation between the thinking and the being: mind (soul) and body are of radically different natures that we are intending to bridge by connecting both aspects in a holistic integration.

The thinking relates to how we process the information we take in. When we acquire knowledge, we construct meaning by connecting fresh data with pre-existing information. At a neurological level, new paths link these data with what we know, establishing connections associated with memories, previous experiences, prior thoughts, familiar images; the new data is also colored by our mostly unconscious associations and emotions. Think of a Google search that brings up 130,000 results in a fraction of a second, based on the whole or partial phrase we typed in. In a similar way, within a fraction of a second, our brain makes millions of simultaneous connections. With such an overflow of information, our rational brain's role is to provide much-needed order: In a millisecond, information is organized in logical and linear sequences, helping us make meaning of the incoming data. Nonrational elements are set aside, and if we succeed in this process, we will feel we "understood" it. If not, we will look perplexed and confused, because we were not able to organize the information. Our way of processing is partly a physical function, partly a learned one. Our schooling system, for example, may reward analytical connections and logical statements—the same way a child brought up in the midst of a rainforest will find rewards in making intuitive connections and learning to connect with the hunted animals or the trees, or a young person raised in an artistic environment will be rewarded for her creative and nonlogical perspectives. For most of our Western-influenced cultures, rational and logical thinking is most fostered and recognized (McGilchrist, 2019).

This prioritization of the rational mind influences how we organize our behaviors, as well as the worldviews we have collectively promoted and replicated, and upon which we are used to act. This way of processing is linear, and in seeking to minimize uncertainty and risk, relies heavily on the need to control the external world; sees one-way connections; and tends to focus on the visible short-term, cause-effect relations. Based on a culturally transmitted tradition of segmentation, we tend to break information into separate elements, in order to subject them to analysis. Conspicuously, this way of process-ing leaves out nonrational data, such as emotions, affect, intuitive knowledge, nonverbal information, paradoxes, contradictory information, spiritual or transcendent embodied experiences, and collective wisdom.

The predominance of rational and analytical thinking has fostered the development of science and technology, with great benefit to humanity's health, comfort, longevity, and entertainment. At the same time, insufficient attention to nonrational information has generated disequilibrium, with the consequent loss of complementary wisdom that can enrich our decisions and behaviors. In other words, when we limit our decisions to "rational" thinking, we lose the emotional and intuitive wisdom that could help in our decisions. When we focus on analytical thinking, we break down reality into discrete parts, and can lose the perspective of the whole. When we are guided solely by linear thinking, we have no insight into the complexity of an interconnected world, with its multiple feedback loops, diverse stakeholders, and cyclical flows. When we concentrate on the relations we can see, we focus on the short term and fail to grasp the larger picture of the long-term impacts of our behaviors or decisions.

This leads us to the next part of the definition.

A way of thinking and being *that results from a broad understanding of the ecosystem's manifestations...*

Our misbalanced way of approaching reality shapes the paradigm we share, which is the foundation of our actions. The results and consequences are visible all around us. Production and consumption patterns adopted 30 or 40 years ago are showing their effect today in the CO_2 levels accumulated in the atmosphere, which can only make us wonder what today's lifestyle will mean for the CO_2 levels 20 years into the future. The CO_2 levels are linked with weather pattern changes and climate-related events like droughts, floods, and fires, which, in turn, have high economic costs for individuals and communities.

One of the challenges of the overwhelming amount of information available to us at every moment of the day is the difficulty to see these changes not only as isolated facts, but to ponder if and how the separate events may be linked. Our automatic processing system is to take in information in silos, and unless we pause to reflect, we may fail to realize that there are feedback loops, that seemingly distant or unrelated events are indeed connected and may serve as catalysts in each other's occurrence. Conditioned as we are to focusing on the visible, linear, short-term, cause-effect relationships, we miss out on the multicausality, on the paradoxes—in short, on the complexity of reality, and as we disregard this complexity, so are our decisions weakened, causing unintentional impacts down the road. For example, we tend to see either-or options: Either profit or planet; either my way or your way; either funds for technology investments or for employees' health plans; either protecting our family or acting for what's best for the community. These either-or options lead to narrow solutions that disregard the wider impacts of our decisions, and those impacts are of great consequence to our planet.

So, *the broad understanding of the ecosystem's manifestations* refers to the importance of seeing what is: The complexity and large picture of our social and environmental reality. By seeing the large picture, from a bird's eye view, we are able to connect the silos and notice links and interconnections. We are able to identify the nonlinear impacts, the mutual influences, and the cyclical flow present in Nature—and realize that humans and all their activities are part of and embedded in Nature. We are able to notice—and learn from—the complexity of paradoxes, to address the scope of impacts beyond the visible moment, and to acknowledge that there has been information that we had been blind to, which takes us to the next section of the definition.

A way of thinking and being that results from a broad understanding of the ecosystem's manifestations, *from social sensitivity...*

By limiting ourselves to the rational processing of information, we disconnect it from any emotional response we might have. We can recite facts about migrations and poverty, the economic impact of climate change, or how unemployment increases due to automation without experiencing any of the stress that would be triggered if we engaged our feelings. However, research indicates that the strictly intellectual approach to sustainability problems also creates a weaker commitment to action (Gifford, 2011; Weber, 2006). If it "makes sense," we feel comfortable acting, but only for as long as it makes sense (or cents). Many environmental actions at the corporate level are based on this sterile and narrow approach, with the danger that they may be discontinued as soon as circumstances change, when corporate priorities shift, and when taking "green" actions appears less relevant. In contradistinction, studies have revealed that shifts in how we see ourselves and our role in the world result in high levels of personal engagement due to the emotional fuel connected to the awareness. This more profound and holistic engagement results in higher motivation to act and to persist in the face of obstacles (Maiteny, 2002; Shrivastava, 2010).

For this reason, the definition names *social sensitivity* as a core component of the Sustainability Mindset, which results from exploring the personal meaning of facts and information. What personal meaning might we have to a profoundly disturbing finding in a 2016 Ellen MacArthur Foundation study that predicted "oceans will contain **more plastic than fish** by 2050 if no actions are taken to reduce the flow of plastics into waterways?[2]" Do we or our colleagues pause and ask: What does this mean for me? How does this fact relate to me, my life, my ancestors, my children? How does it make me feel? By connecting facts with our personal affects and emotional responses, we are able to develop a more complex and holistic understanding of the information, at the same time that we engage more fully with it. The exploration of our feelings is closely connected with a question that logically follows: How am I contributing to this problem?—which leads us to the next section of the definition.

A way of thinking and being that results from a broad understanding of the ecosystem's manifestations, from social sensitivity, *as well as an introspective focus on one's personal values…*

In my study, exploring the motivations of business leaders championing sustainability initiatives in their organizations, several individuals interviewed indicated that significant moments in their mindset shift arose when they looked at facts and asked themselves: How are WE contributing to this? And their sudden realization: We are part of this problem, we are creating it! The thought rapidly moved to their personal contribution: I am not a bad person, yet I am contributing to this situation…! (Rimanoczy, 2010).

The realization that we are playing an (unintentional) role in the problems is a powerful insight. It leads us to revise our values, to question what we stand for and to inquire how are we living up to our stated or held values. The study gave evidence that by scrutinizing our daily habits and behaviors, we come to see how they are the result of unexplored anchors of our identity. It is a powerful insight—also frequently accompanied by an equally powerful urge to rationalize one's behavior.

For example, a student in my MBA class was watching a video about inhumane industrial food processing in the agribusiness field. Instead of reading about it, which would have allowed him to maintain his emotional distance, he watched images of overcrowded corn-feeding cattle stations and chicken processing plants. He felt terrible and suddenly looked down to his plate, noticing that he was eating chicken nuggets. He realized that he was contributing, albeit unintentionally, to the problem. Then, at the same time that he felt badly, he had this justifying thought: Well, I am working hard and late, and I don't have time to cook, so a fast-food option is a solution that helps me continue being productive in my work. On further reflection, he realized that for him, work productivity meant a possible promotion and a better salary, i.e., the road to success, which was an important value for him. He also realized that comfort (in this case, fast food) was another important value, taking automatic priority over more environmentally sound habits. This awareness path led the student from information, to emotions, to connecting the dots, to seeing his personal contribution to the problems, to scrutinizing his habits and values, to questioning the anchors of his identity.

This expansion of self-awareness is possible when we pause, reflect, and develop the habit of an introspective focus. *Who am I?* is a profound question that easily emerges when we create a space for it and it leads us to the next part of the definition.

"A way of thinking and being that results from a broad understanding of the ecosystem's manifestations, from social sensitivity, as well as an introspective focus on one's personal values *and higher self…* "

In our fast-paced world, we are all challenged by a never-ending to-do list, and technology has only worsened the expectations: If a WhatsApp or a WeChat message is not answered by the end of the day, something must be wrong. As a spontaneous coping mechanism, we divide our attention among many simultaneous demands, thereby providing more superficial and automatic responses. Except for serious or legal situations, most of the time we are not expected to pause, reflect, write a draft, revise it, wait some time, then read it again, and revise it again before we send it out. Our automatic behaviors make us efficient and save time: When we drive we can be solving a problem mentally; when we answer a question, we can be mentally planning what we will do next; etc. The downside of our automatic behaviors comes when we don't realize that our actions are supporting values we really don't agree with. For the student, his automatic behavior was to prioritize comfort, and the unscrutinized part was that by doing so he was supporting the inhumane management of animals. The moment he paused and made that connection, he felt badly—not just for the animals, but now about himself. His self-image as a virtuous, good person was dented by the realization that he was actually behaving in a way he didn't approve of himself. This moment of cognitive dissonance creates a tension as we experience the painful gap (for our ego) between on the one hand, who we want to be and how we want to live up to the best version of ourselves, and on the other hand, our own actions.

When we realize that gap, we may be also raising other related questions: So what is my purpose, anyway? Why am I here, in this job, in this class, in this world? What is my mission, if I have one? How am I expressing my higher values, my higher self? All these questions can emerge when we pause, make a space to reflect, and also when we engage in contemplative practices, such as meditation in its different shapes and forms. This is a powerful component of the Sustainability Mindset, which connects the individual with his transcendent aspects, his religious or secular spirituality; expands the frontiers of self; and creates experiences of otherness and oneness with all that is.

The cognitive dissonance at the same time is a powerful source of energy that propels us to action, to do something, which leads us finally to the last part completing the definition of a Sustainability Mindset.

A way of thinking and being that results from a broad understanding of the ecosystem's manifestations, from social sensitivity, as well as an introspective focus on one's personal values and higher self, *and finds its expression in actions for the greater good of the whole*

In my interviews with leaders who were engaged in reshaping their business toward social or environmental positive actions, I repeatedly observed a sequence. They came in touch with information, connected the dots, realized in shock they were personally contributing to the problems, felt emotional, questioned their purpose and values, and finally had the urge to act. "I need to do something, I need to share this with others, I cannot be the only one seeing this." This sequence was later observed with students participating in the Sustainability Mindset course in different locations. The path from social sensitivity to the need to act has been equally described in the literature (Batson, 2010; Brown et al, 2019; Daloz, Keen, Keen, Park, 1996; Rimanoczy, 2010).

The leaders I studied were selected by a criterion that certainly conditioned the results: I only studied individuals who took effective actions in their organizations. There may be cases where individuals making those connections feel overwhelmed, cannot tolerate the cognitive dissonance, and opt for other ways to solve the tension. These can include indifference, denial, sticking to more superficial topics, avoidance, focusing on more materialistic goals, and/or concentrating exclusively on *doing* at the expense of cultivating their holistic *being*.

Seeking to learn from those who had transformed their way of thinking and acted in new, sustainable ways, I studied the components of their Sustainability Mindset in order to identify how they could be best developed intentionally.

Developing a Sustainability Mindset

After listing the core elements that could be intentionally developed, it became clear that they fell into specific content areas: Ecological Worldview (related to understanding the state of the planet and how we feel about it); Systems Perspective (processing information using a systemic lens); Emotional Intelligence (particularly introspective practices to increase self-awareness and explore personal values); and Spiritual Intelligence (relating to questions of purpose, transcendence, and oneness). I anchored these different content areas in the syllabus on a collaborative project to make a difference, which provided the opportunity for students to channel their feelings and energy into some tangible action (See Figure 1.3).[3]

This framework has been used since 2010 in different courses and modules around the world to develop a mindset for sustainability. The many iterations and input from faculty members of the PRME Working Group on the

Figure 1.3 Content areas of the Sustainability Mindset course

Source: Adapted from Rimanoczy (2016).

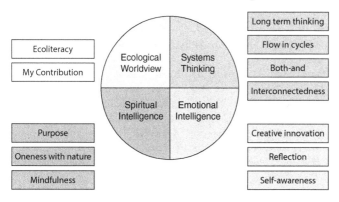

Figure 1.4 The 12 Sustainability Mindset Principles and the 4 content areas

Sustainability Mindset, in over 46 countries, led to the identification and statement of 12 Principles. Figure 1.4 presents the 12 Sustainability Mindset Principles and how they correspond to the 4 content areas of the framework.

In the next chapters each Principle will be introduced.

Notes

1. https://www.un.org/development/desa/en/news/statistics/ energy-tracking-report.html; https://www.un.org/sustainable development/progress-report/ Retrieved January 26 2019.
2. Source:https://www.ellenmacarthurfoundation.org/publications/ the-new-plastics-economy-rethinking-the-future-of-plastics.
3. This model was further elaborated by Kassel, Rimanoczy & Mitchell, connecting different aspects with the knowing being and doing dimensions (2018, pp.3–37).

References

Batson, C. D. (2010). Empathy-induced altruistic motivation. In M. Mikulincer & P. R. Shaver.. (Eds.), *Prosocial motives, emotions, and behavior: The better angels of our nature* (pp. 15–34). Washington, D.C.: American Psychological Association. Retrieved from https://doi.org/10.1037/12061-001. Accessed March 8, 2020.

Brown, K., Adger, W. N., Devine-Wright, P., Anderies, J. M., Barr, S., Bousquet, F., & Quinn, T. (2019). Empathy, place and identity interactions for sustainability. *Global Environmental Change, 56*, 11–17.

Daloz, L. A. P., Keen, C. H., Keen, J. P., & Parks, S. D. (1996). Lives of commitment Higher education in the life of the new commons. *Change: The Magazine of Higher Learning, 28*(3), 10–15.

Elgin, D. (2009). *The living universe: Where are we? Who are we? Where are we going?* San Francisco, CA: Berrett Koehler Publisher.

Gifford, R. (2011). The dragons of inaction: Psychological barriers that limit climate change mitigation and adaptation. *American Psychologist, 66*(4), 290.

Kassel, K., Rimanoczy, I., & Mitchell, S. F. (2018). A sustainability mindset model for management education. In K. Kassel & I. Rimanoczy. (Eds.), *Developing a sustainability mindset in management education*, (3–37). London: Routledge.

Kumar, S. (2002). You are therefore I am. *A declaration of dependence* (p. 107). Cambridge, UK: Green Books.

Maiteny, P. (2002). Mind in the gap: Summary of research exploring 'inner' influences on pro-sustainability learning and behaviour. *Environmental Education Research, 8*(3), 299–306. doi:10.1080/13504620220145447.

McGilchrist, I. (2019). *The master and his emissary: The divided brain and the making of the western world.* New Haven, CT: Yale University Press.

Meadows, D. (1997). Places to intervene in a system. *Whole Earth, 91*(1), 78–84.

Rimanoczy, I. B. (2010). *Business leaders committing to and fostering sustainability initiatives* (Doctoral dissertation). Teachers College, Columbia University.

Rimanoczy, I. (2016). A holistic learning approach for responsible management education. In R. Sunley & J. Leigh. (Eds.), *Educating for responsible management: Putting theory into practice* (pp. 159–184). Sheffield, UK: Greenleaf Publishing.

Shrivastava, P. (2010). Pedagogy of passion for sustainability. *Academy of Management Learning & Education, 9*(3), 443–455.

Smith, P. A. & Sharicz, C. (2011). The shift needed for sustainability. *The Learning Organization: An International Journal, 18*(1), 73–86.

Speth, J. G. (2009). *The bridge at the edge of the world: Capitalism, the environment, and crossing from crisis to sustainability* (p. 204). New Haven, CT: Yale University Press.

Tsao, F. C., & Laszlo, C. (2019). *Quantum leadership: New consciousness in business*. Palo Alto, CA: Stanford University Press.

Wamsler, C. & Brink, E. (2018). Mindsets for sustainability: Exploring the link between mindfulness and sustainable climate adaptation. *Ecological Economics*, *151*, 55–61.

Weber, E. U. (2006). Experience-based and description-based perceptions of long-term risk: Why global warming does not scare us (yet). *Climatic Change*, 77(1–2), 103–120.

Wilber, K. (2005). Introduction to integral theory and practice. *AQAL: Journal of Integral Theory and Practice*, 1(1), 2–38.

Part II

Ecological Worldview

This part starts with the content area of *Ecological Worldview*. In the original research that prompted the concept of a Sustainability Mindset, several business leaders interviewed showed a similar sequence in their process of shifting their perspectives. At some point and under different circumstances, they were confronted with information about environmental, social, or health-related problems that were indirectly linked to their business or industry. They were not unaware of those problems, but they just had never made the connection to how they personally played a role in this. In some cases, it was very specific information, for example, the role of someone in the food industry in the negative long-term health implications of processed food or the role of a technology corporation in the slow contamination of soil due to industrial waste pollution. In other cases, it was a more wide-ranging perspective, for example, realizing the complex connections of consumption patterns to weather-related events, deforestation, and increased volume of natural resources use. None of the individuals studied was actually part of any illegal operation or violating existing regulations. But it is well known that legislation always lags behind the circumstances, and the long-term impacts of business practices are not always considered if they are even measured or studied.

This stage of seeing a larger picture was a very important moment in their awakening journey, particularly as they asked themselves in how many ways they were (unintentionally) contributing to the problems. This created a tension between their values and what they realized were the "values in action," and this cognitive dissonance was a very powerful motivator to take action.

When designing the syllabus to develop a Sustainability Mindset, I intentionally replicated that sequence and started providing the students with a broad picture of the state of the planet, prompting them to explore their feelings and also to identify in what ways they were personally contributing to the problems.

The content area of Ecological Worldview, thus, includes the Principles of *Ecoliteracy* and *My Contribution* as key steps in the development of a Sustainability Mindset.

2 Principle number 1
Ecoliteracy

Definition
Understanding the state of the planet allows us to be more fully aware of the challenges, the complexity of how they are linked to each other, and to explore what it means to us.
Teaching Goal
Students understand the state of the planet, the interconnections, and what it means for them.
Meta Goal
To become aware of the global situation and personally engaged.

Origins of the Principle

My research studying the factors that influenced a mindset shift in leaders as they became aware of the environmental and/or social impacts of their behaviors or decisions showed that their sudden understanding of the broad spectrum of planetary challenges was a key factor. It played a role in the motivational impulses to engage in sustainability actions, either seeking to correct "unsustainable" practices, stopping environmentally harmful behaviors, or looking for innovations in rethinking their business practices (Hermes & Rimanoczy, 2018; Rimanoczy, 2010, 2019). A leader of an international fast food corporation observed that when he realized the magnitude of these problems, he wanted "to shoot myself…"; and the late industrialist and corporate responsibility champion, Ray Anderson, publicly described this moment as "a spear through the heart." It was not only their realization of the impacts of their business practices (something that today we are more aware of), but particularly their glimpse into the magnitude of and systemic connections between their different behaviors and the consequences.

Some authors suggest the importance of ecoliteracy connecting personally with an individual. The awareness of global problems cannot be limited to just cognitive information without emotional content (Kineman & Poli, 2014). Individuals can move on a continuum from awareness to appreciation, to knowledge and understanding, to personal responsibility, and finally to action (Barnes, 2013, cited by Lees, 2017). Others promote cognitive and affective learning for an ecological intelligence (Goleman, Bennett, & Barlow, 2012) that connects head, heart, hands, and spirit (Stone, 2010).

We are citing and adapting here the concept of ecoliteracy that distinguishes the following components (Kim, Vaswani, Kang, Nam, & Lee, 2017):

- Scientific understanding of environmental or ecological processes and patterns.
- Grasp of ecological connectivity.
- Appreciation for the connections between ecological and social systems (Jordan, Singer, Vaughan, & Berkowitz, 2009; Nadasdy, 1999; Reynolds & Lowman, 2013).
- Making new meaning on a personal level and acknowledging the emotional impact of the information.

Why do we need this Principle?

Certainly, awareness of our planetary challenges has been rapidly expanding over the past decade, due to the unfortunate reality of increasingly tragic weather-related events: Storms, fires out of control, flooding, droughts, and changes in climate patterns affecting harvests. All have had serious impacts on the economies and health of millions around the globe. Human behavior and neglect accumulated over time have resulted in waste, depletion of natural resources, pollution, and contamination of land and water. Further, social challenges, related or unrelated to climate conditions, such as human migrations, struggles for human rights, impact of technology, and effect of poverty are part of the current landscape. The media provides daily coverage, and in direct or indirect ways educates the population on the linkages between human behaviors and the challenges we face, such as the connections between pervasive use of plastic and the microplastics that contaminate waterways and leach into our food chain. Students are increasingly aware of both the local challenges and the global ones, and in 2020, COVID-19 came to give us an experiential learning on many levels. One of them was that when humans were quarantined, Nature blossomed, and megacities in China saw a blue sky again, while swans came back into the Venetian canals.

If this is the case, then why is the Principle of Ecoliteracy needed for developing a Sustainability Mindset?

The distinction made in this Principle is in the *transdisciplinary approach* to ecoliteracy, and in the *focus,* which goes beyond mere intellectual understanding. Orr (1992; 2004) suggested a transdisciplinary approach toward ecoliteracy education. His visionary perspective is adopted here since the value of this Principle is in its broad application. It is not restricted to the specifics of any discipline, because the transdisciplinary approach provides a wide encompassing perspective without necessarily going in depth into any field. Individuals may be more versed in one area or another, but here the purpose is to offer a birds-eye view that makes evident the *magnitude and complexity* of the challenges. For example, a meteorologist understands the weather challenges caused by destructive human activities and social scientists understand the poverty challenges also caused by human activities. A transdisciplinary approach doesn't differentiate between the disciplines of meteorology or social science, and looks at the problems through a holistic lens.

Furthermore, ecoliteracy here aims at highlighting the connections between what we tend to see as isolated events; through ecoliteracy, we learn the feedback loops that are at play, whether they are known (such as the impact of rainforest destruction on the release of captured CO_2) or whether they are estimated (i.e., what will be the impact of the methane columns emerging from the permafrost melting in the Arctic).

Finally, the focus is to link data with meaning, to go beyond merely cognitive learning. To engage the whole being, feelings must be brought into the classroom. "One in six individuals doesn't have access to clean drinking water" is a scientific statement. We can memorize and cite it. To engage the whole individual, we have to build linkages with the emotions and the personal context of each individual, to make it relevant for them, asking questions like "What does this mean for you? How do you feel when you read this, and why?" (Vargas–Madrazo, 2018).

How is this Principle effectively brought into the classroom?

Each Principle is brought to the classroom via a concrete Teaching Goal. This is a goal that can be brought into the classroom plan without difficulty, independently of the subject taught.

The power of this Principle is best stated in the **Teaching Goal:**

> *Students understand the state of the planet and the interconnections, and what it means for them.*

In addition, each Principle has a *Meta Goal*, which is a "wishful" goal, something that in the best case may also be attained.

Meta Goal:

> *To become aware of the global situation, and personally engaged.*

As previously indicated, the goal is to feature breadth rather than depth of understanding and a different perspective in the context of an education that is currently organized into siloed disciplines. By helping students get a glimpse into the complex landscape of social and environmental challenges, we introduce them to the many aspects of our reality. While some may doubt climate science, there is a multitude of other nonclimate related problems that students must acknowledge as part of the world in which they operate. This information is to be accompanied by an exploration of the feelings it elicits in each individual so that it contributes to a more holistic learning experience.

The Meta Goal, more ambitious, is that not only become the students aware of the situation, but that the connections with their own emotions make them personally engaged. This is a more lasting result and it will have positive consequences in their decisions and daily behaviors.

Key components

Key components are leverage points that can accelerate achieving the Teaching Goal of a Principle. The key components to be covered in this Principle are water, energy, soil, air, biodiversity, and social aspects. In brief, their related aspects cover:

> Water: health of rivers and oceans, pollution, melting glaciers, drought, decreases in drinking water, sea level rise;

Energy: CO_2, global warming, climate change, weather-related events;

Soil: desertification, contamination, biodiversity loss;

Air: pollution;

Biodiversity: species extinction, depletion of natural resources;

Social Aspects: inequity in all its multiple forms, hunger, health, conflict and war, waste of resources, automation's impact on labor, migration.

Note that these aspects relate to the challenges, not to the solutions that are being developed to address them. While solutions can be part of the conversation, it is recommended that they not be used to mitigate the seriousness of the challenges; it is critical not to ignore our emotions or feelings by diverting our attention toward less painful thoughts. This is a common behavior, a way to minimize stress or painful feelings; and while it can rapidly move into proactive behaviors—"let me do something"—it can prevent us from acknowledging the emotional connections we experience as we confront unwelcome information. The danger is that information induces a purely cognitive reaction, thus making it an intellectual problem to be solved. People who focus only on facts stay "safe" from any holistic experiences that might connect the problem with themselves. This comes at the price of slowing one's personal development into more expanded levels of consciousness.

There will be opportunities to discuss innovations and initiatives to address particular challenges, but it should be remembered that the teaching goal of this Principle is to get a broad picture of our planetary challenges, and the feelings we experience as we acknowledge them.

Once the broad spectrum of challenges and the concomitant feelings have been identified and discussed, the educator can take the next step, which is to introduce the conversation about what solutions, innovations, activism campaigns, or movements are underway to address the challenges. All these options help mitigate the audience's emotional reactions and can serve to lessen a feeling of being overwhelmed. This is important because awareness of the dire challenges can easily generate feelings of help-lessness, which, in turn, can launch defensive mechanisms such as denial, indifference, saturation, and neglect, even depression and addictive behaviors of distraction (Doherty & Clayton, 2011; Fritze, Blashki, Burke, & Wiseman, 2008; Weber, 2010).

Juxtaposing these possibilities for addressing serious challenges can provide inspiration and hope. It also may be used as the trigger to participants to select for themselves a project that will make a difference. Stone (2017) cites the case of a school teacher who shared with her fourth-graders a film about the rainforest destruction. The students were distressed and asked her what they could do. She invited them to find a species and study it, and they would fall in love with it. The thinking behind this suggestion was that we love and are motivated to take care of what we understand.

Preparing yourself for the task

As educators step from their more familiar role of teaching a subject to the new task of facilitating the development of a Sustainability Mindset, they may welcome guidance to prepare their curriculum so that they feel organized and grounded. This preparation relates not only to materials and possible exercises, but actually starts with expanding one's own self-awareness, since the internal aspects of the mindset will touch the educator as much as the students.

For this reason, we offer a set of Key Questions for the educator, inviting you to pause, reflect, and perhaps use journaling to explore questions that may be new for you.

Key questions for the educator are as follows:

For self-awareness:

- What do these facts mean for me, and how do they make me feel?
- How do I deal with these emotions?
- How might I respond to them more effectively?
- In what ways could I convert the feelings into pro-active behaviors?

To prepare the assignments/activities:

- What does my audience know?
- What is the most recent information and most recent research available?
- What is still missing for me?
- What is the understanding of the audience of the interconnections and feedback loops?
- What may each of these facts mean personally to each individual of the audience?

Tips for the educator:

- Provide **place-specific information**: It is easier to make information relevant and engaging if it relates to the location of the school, city, state, region, or country. For international audiences, seek data relevant to their different countries of origin or residence.
- Provide **industry- or profession-specific information**: When addressing water, soil, or social issues, connections to the audience's discipline will help bring relevance. For example, data about sanitation challenges may be linked in a different way for engineering or architecture students, or for health professionals. Connections to inequity facts will be of a different but important relevance to economists, social workers, or lawyers. Help create the bridges that will increase the relevance to, and engagement of, the students.

- Seek **experiential learning**: Assign students to conduct real interviews with someone affected by some of the circumstances included in the lesson plan; have them collect testimonials, engage a guest speaker who can tell a real story; organize site visits to a landfill to have a first-hand experience of what happens to objects that we discard, or visits to an inner city neighborhood, a farm, etc.
- Second best (after first-hand experiences) are **videos**: They provide an opportunity to connect emotionally, albeit not in the presence of another person and without the power of a holistic real-life encounter.
- Third best are **images** in addition to text: Text and data should accompany and illustrate images, and not the other way around. The image provides the audience a more powerful message than the cognitive facts, therefore better facilitating the exploration of associated feelings.
- Engage your students in **activities that show or allow to draw links** between events and feedback loops.
- Engage your students in activities or **questions to prompt a personal meaning** of the data.
- Link problems and solutions to **behaviors** and possibilities.
- Link problems and solutions to the Sustainable Development Goals and targets.

An exercise to try out

For this Principle, powerful exercises can be designed for an "*in their shoes*" experience to develop social sensitivity and empathic understanding. This could be, for example, an interview with a person who is affected by one of the environmental or social challenges; following or accompanying that person for some period of time in what is their routine; participating in an activity but not in the role of volunteer but from the receiving side (i.e., by begging, being fed at a soup kitchen, etc.); walking, as a woman, into a place where it is obligatory to have your head covered.

A story

Prof Amelia Naim Indrajaya teaches at a privileged business school in Jakarta, Indonesia. One assignment had the students accompany some scavengers in the city. They walked during several hours with the person while she/he was picking up garbage that could be sold at the end of the day. The students were tired after walking so many hours, and shocked at how little money the people received after their big effort. Their worldview changed with that single experience, which had an impact in how they saw poverty and pay differences—and in some cases impacted the salary paid by their family's business to their workers. They developed social sensitivity in a holistic way that would never have been achieved by sharing statistics of poverty.

Other resources

Celedonia, K. L. & Rosenthal, A. T. (2011). Combining art and eco-literacy to reconnect urban communities to nature. *Ecopsychology, 3*(4), 249–255.

Dewberry, E. (2018). Eco-literacy in Transition: The role of design ecologies in developing our capacity for radical change. In *Can Design Catalyse the Great Transition? Papers from the Transition Design Symposium 2016* (pp. 127–136). The School of Design at Carnegie Mellon University, Schumacher College and the New Weather Institute, UK.

Fields, T. R. (2014). "We ain't got no wildlife here": Transformative effects of a contemplative assignment in ecoliteracy. *Naropa Green Papers.* https://www.naropa.edu/documents/programs/ma-environmental-leadership/fields-green-paper.pdf

Inclezan, D. & Pradanos, L. (2014). Promoting ecoliteracy in an introductory database systems course: Activities for the first week. In *Proceedings of the 45th ACM technical symposium on computer science education* (pp. 573–578). ACM. https://dl.acm.org/doi/proceedings/10.1145/2538862

Madden, L. & Dell'Angelo, T. (2016). Using photojournals to develop ecoliteracy in a blended environmental science course. *Journal of College Science Teaching*, *46*(1), 26. https://www.ecoliteracy.org/article/teaching-strategies

References

Barnes, J. C. (2013). Awareness to action: The journey toward a deeper ecological literacy. *Journal of Sustainability Education*, *5*(5), 1–5. Retrieved from http://www.journalofsustainabilityeducation.org/

Doherty, T. J. & Clayton, S. (2011). The psychological impacts of global climate change. *American Psychologist*, *66*(4), 265.

Fritze, J. G., Blashki, G. A., Burke, S., & Wiseman, J. (2008). Hope, despair and transformation: Climate change and the promotion of mental health and wellbeing. *International Journal of Mental Health Systems*, *2*(1), 13.

Goleman, D., Bennett, L., & Barlow, Z. (2012). *Ecoliterate: How educators are cultivating emotional, social and ecological intelligence*. San Francisco, CA: Jossey-Bass.

Hermes, J. & Rimanoczy, I. (2018). Deep learning for a sustainability mindset. *The International Journal of Management Education*, *16*(3), 460–467.

Jordan, R., Singer, F., Vaughan, J., & Berkowitz, A. (2018). What should every citizen know about ecology? *Frontiers in Ecology and the Environment*, *7*, 495–500.

Kim, G., Vaswani, R., Kang, W., Nam, M., & Lee, D. (2017). Enhancing ecoliteracy through traditional ecological knowledge in proverbs. *Sustainability*, *9*(7), 1182.

Kineman, J. J. & Poli, R. (2014). Ecological literacy leadership: Into the mind of nature. *Bulletin of the Ecological Society of America*, *95*(1), 30–58. doi:10.1890/0012- 9623-95.1.30.

Lees, M. V. (2017). *Effect of contemplative pedagogy on the ecoliteracy of undergraduate public state university students* (Doctoral dissertation). Walden University, Minneapolis, MN.

Nadasdy, P. (1999). The politics of Tek: Power and the "integration" of knowledge. *Arctic Anthropology*, *36*, 1–18.

Orr, D. W. (1992). *Ecological literacy: Education and the transition to a postmodern world*. Albany, NY: Suny Press.

Orr, D. W. (2004). *Earth in mind: On education, environment, and the human prospect*. Washington, DC: Island Press.

Reynolds, J. A., Lowman, M. D. (2010). Promoting ecoliteracy through research service-learning and citizen science. *Frontiers in Ecology and the Environment, 11*, 565–566.

Rimanoczy, I. B. (2010). *Business leaders committing to and fostering sustainability initiatives* (Doctoral dissertation). Teachers College, Columbia University.

Rimanoczy, I. (2019). Personal development toward a sustainability mindset. In Radha Sharma (Ed.) *Human resource management for organizational sustainability* (pp. 19–32). New York, NY: Business Expert Press.

Stone, M. (2010). A schooling for sustainability framework. *Teacher Education Quarterly, 37*(4), 33–46.

Stone, M. K. (2017). Ecoliteracy and schooling for sustainability. In JSTOR (Ed.) *EarthEd* (pp. 35–47). Washington, DC: Island Press.

Vargas-Madrazo, E. (2018). Contemplative dialogue as the basis for a transdisciplinary attitude: Ecoliteracy toward an education for human sustainability. *World Futures, 74*(4), 224–245.

Weber, E. U. (2010). What shapes perceptions of climate change? *Wiley Interdisciplinary Reviews: Climate Change, 1*(3), 332–342.

3 Principle number 2

My contribution

Definition
When we identify the ways in which we are unintentionally contributing to the problems, we have a chance to do
something about them. It also expands our consciousness
and develops social sensitivity.
Teaching Goal
*Students identify the ways in which they personally contribute to
the problems.*
Meta Goal
*To develop the habit of always seeking our unintentional
contribution.*

Origins of the Principle

I started my exploratory study to understand the motivations of leaders who championed sustainability initiatives,
with the aim of identifying the *one* reason or the major
moment that had launched their personal transformation.
The study showed, however, that they didn't cite one specific moment as pivotal to their mindset shift, but instead
articulated a series of significant moments that had, increasingly, prompted a transformation in their behaviors.

One of those turning points mentioned repeatedly by
several individuals had taken place after they had been
made aware of the links between human behaviors and

our planetary challenges, and particularly after they were able to get in touch with their own feelings of sadness, concern, compassion, or bewilderment. This led them to wonder how their own industry might be responsible for some of the problems, and from there, it was just a small step for them to ask themselves: *And how am I contributing to this?* They pondered their own role in the decisions the organization had been taking, whether strategic or technical. In some cases, they also became conscious of the effect of their domestic habits on the environment, but in most cases, their inquiry focused on corporate behaviors, which were of a much larger impact (Rimanoczy, 2010).

As they did this, they connected external events with their personal values and their sense of self and identity and also with how they wanted to see themselves—their ethical or moral self-image. It became clear to them that regardless of the fact that their contributions to the problems had been unintentional, their actions (or inactions) had created impacts they would not, in good conscience, accept as a cost of doing business. They stated it in different ways ("I am not a bad person!" "I have children", "I have grandchildren") and they imagined how they would question their behaviors someday in the future. Although the change in awareness didn't happen instantly, to these leaders, the thought of the values they were communicating by way of their behaviors became a recurring preoccupation, as they found they couldn't match their "values in action" with their espoused values (Argyris, 1980; Argyris & Schon, 1974). This resulted in a cognitive dissonance, a tension that persisted. And while it was not always shared with others and remained an intimate struggle, it eventually prompted them to do something to end such an emotionally stressful situation. "I had to do something!" was a phrase heard repeatedly throughout the study.

Research points to the importance of going beyond ethical, normative, and economic decision-making models when seeking to elicit sustainable behaviors. Moral emotions and other psychological non-rational elements have a strong impact on leaders (Holmberg, 2014; Sekerka & Stimel, 2012; Starik, 2004). Various studies have identified guilt feelings in connection with sustainability. For example, in the area of responsible consumer behaviors, guilt and pride have been found as powerful motivators for consumers' sustainable choices (Antonetti & Maklan 2014; Jayaratne, Sullivan Mort, & Clare, 2015; Kals & Maes, 2002; Onwezen, Bartels, & Antonides, 2014). At the same time, the motivational power of guilt and other negative emotions, such as sadness and despair, has been questioned by some authors (Sekerka & Stimel, 2012) who suggest, for example, avoiding them with students and promoting positive feelings of agency and hope instead. Positive psychology has argued that uplifting feelings like hope, opportunity, and satisfaction are much better motivators than negative emotions (O'Brien, 2012; Stir, 2006; Verdugo, 2012). Furthermore, while some welcome projections, warnings, and doomsday scenarios as necessary wake-up calls, such as the youth movements Extinction Rebellion and Fridays for Future and other youth movements inspired by Greta Thunberg (Gunningham, 2019; Kühne, 2019; Murray, 2020), others criticize the focus on dramatic future scenarios (Cross, 1998; Swyngedouw, 2013).

Why do we need this Principle?

Independent of the academic positions, the cognitive dissonance of the leaders in my study became a key step in the evolution of their mindset. The tension of misalignment between their self-image and the consequences of their decisions was a powerful force in moving them to action. The movement toward taking action must be a goal in sustainability education, and we have here a compelling stimulus to initiate movement among students: The simple inquiry into what is each person's contribution to the problems that concern us deeply.

In view of this, in the course designed to develop a sustainability mindset, students are not only exposed to information about planetary challenges, and are invited to explore their feelings, but also prompted to identify the ways in which they are personally contributing to the problems. To balance the negative emotions, and possible feelings of helplessness, educators can provide concrete opportunities to make a difference and guide students to minimize the tensions by taking the decision to "get into real action." Also, educators can guide the conversation toward the positive, altruistic behaviors that the students may have shown during the COVID-19 crisis.

How is this Principle effectively brought into the classroom?

The power of this Principle is best stated in the **Teaching Goal:**

> *Students identify the ways in which they are personally contributing to the problems.*

The long-term aspiration of this Principle is best stated in the **Meta Goal:**

> *To develop the habit of always seeking our unintentional contribution.*

When learning about the many challenges humanity faces, it is natural to feel a wide spectrum of emotions. Some individuals just don't like bad news and want to focus on positive things or solutions. Others react with disbelief, or question science, or even entertain conspiracy theories where some elites are seeking to manipulate people's opinions. Others tend to look at governmental inefficiency or corporate mischief, blaming them as the cause of all problems. In any of these reactions, there is a common denominator: It leaves the individual feeling powerless, a victim of something greater than self, and at the mercy of circumstances and decisions outside the individual's control.

This is the paradox of focusing on our personal contribution: It may cause sensitivity and pain, but it actually is the only empowering option. There is a popular anecdote attributed to Pope John XXIII, where he shared that it often happened to him to wake up at night and begin to think about a serious problem, and decide he should tell the Pope about it. Then he would wake up completely and remember "I am the Pope!" When we have the courage to face how we are contributing to significant problems, we realize that we do, indeed, have control over our own decisions and choices.

We are the Pope.

Key components

The key components to be addressed in this Principle are as follows:

- Contributions are made both by doing and by not doing.
- Contributions occur at an individual and a group level.
- We need to shift from unintentional impact to conscious awareness.
- We must establish personal commitment: What will I do?

Contributions result from both doing and not doing, which is an important and not always obvious fact. We may be more used to seek direct ways in which we cause harm. For example, when exploring the problem of biodiversity loss, educators must bear in mind that scenarios in which the loss of biodiversity occurs may seem distant geo-graphically, and thus have no apparent connection to the world of the student. However, after a discussion on the topic in class, a student may take a different look at the front yard in her home, which is well-maintained, protected from weeds, and untidy overgrowth. To keep this neat and manicured lawn requires the application of pesticides, fertilizers, weed-controllers, and regular mowing to a height of 4 inches. While these actions may not be the responsibility of the student, she now may be paying attention if there is any loss of biodiversity happening on the property. She might realize that the focus on cropped foliage and neat flower beds has depressed the number of bees that pollinate the foliage. And it is possible that she will become aware that *not doing* anything about it is in effect contributing to the problem.

Contributions happen at the individual and at the group level, and the levels are often intertwined. Continuing with the previous example, let's say that the student rationalizes that her failure to act is not actually her choice, because she lives in a gated community that has its own regulations on how the yards must look and be maintained. This brings up a new question: How are we at a collective level making a contribution to the problem? What tacit agreement do we have in our Home Owners Association?

The tendency to blame others and to displace responsibility outside oneself is a spontaneous human reaction, as we observed before. Its effect is to put a person into the passenger seat, powerless and at the mercy of the driver. By identifying "collective" contributions, the individual can acknowledge his personal role within the collective, and choose what to do. We all pick our battles, and the essential relevance of this Principle is to understand the importance of, and then move toward attaining, the shift *from unintentional impact to conscious awareness*.

The power of this and the other Principles is that they launch new ways to look at the world, fresh ways to analyze and review information. Like other habits of mind, repetition and reinforcement are important, and over time one question can become part of our thought process: "I wonder how I am contributing to this?"

The educator's key intervention is prompting students to take action by asking them: *"What will* you *do?"* Their response can help channel negative feelings and energy into something positive, and it can give them a sense of agency, control, and influence in shaping the world they would like to live in.

Educators can use the COVID-19 experience, which is very relevant. After identifying the type of negative contribution we are making, they can ask: Did some spontaneous positive behaviors during the COVID-19 crisis reverse or diminish the negative contribution? For example, compulsive consumption may be one of the personal negative contributions to pollution or resource depletion. During the virus crisis, did they miss shopping? How did they feel about not being able to consume as "usual"? By having a dialogue about this very concrete experience, individuals can build upon it and see that behavior change as possible, not a utopic desire.

Preparing yourself for the task

As indicated before, each of these Principles touches not only the students, but also the educators, and ignoring this will make the educators' task stressful or even impossible. On the other hand, when the educators accept the novelty of exploring their own feelings and thoughts on these new perspectives, they engage in an unexpected journey of personal evolution and development.

To facilitate this path of personal discovery, we list here a few key questions for the educator. Pause, reflect, and then add your own thoughts and questions.

Key questions for the educator:

For self-awareness:

- How am I myself modeling this Principle?
- What emotions may be triggered in me? Guilt? Self-criticism? Helplessness?
- What defensive mechanisms do I tend to use? Anger? Blame? "Passing the buck?"
- How can I best deal with these emotions—both the students' and my own?

To prepare the assignments/activities:

- How can I prompt reflection that will link individual behaviors at the personal, professional, and community level? This can happen in the context of their family, friends, organization, or at various political levels.
- How can I introduce the idea that a contribution is the result of both action (by doing) and inaction (by not doing)?
- What are some spurs that can help students to connect with opportunities and possibilities. What have been inspiring cases of what can be done?

Tips for the educator:

- Pay attention to the level of students' maturity in understanding their level of responsibility: Are they focused on meeting just minimal regulations to avoid penalties? Or are they perhaps focused on minimizing harm? Are they at the following stage, which is to *avoid* doing harm? Are they more actively engaged in reducing the usage of resources or perhaps interested in inventing new alternatives? Are some at the highest level, where they seek to lead change and influence others? Acquisition of maturity cannot be forced on someone, but it can be acknowledged, and options can be discussed to expand the horizon of consciousness. Provide opportunities for channeling emotions, thereby converting them into actions.

- Foster interest in students taking action to address issues, however small, in the real world. Institutional education is used to provide case studies, assign problems or projects that students have to analyze and debate, and on which they have to write recommendations or reports. These are good intellectual classroom exercises, but the resulting recommendations or reports rarely if ever get implemented. Taking action to address actual challenges in the real world is a powerful learning experience. Learning by doing confronts students with the complexity of real life, and can provide them with a boost in self-confidence at having achieved something. They learn that they can make a difference.
- Provide inspiration through stories of what is possible.
- Discuss areas of influence and control.
  What do you have control over?
  Where do you have indirect control?
  What are your opportunities to influence decisions?
  We tend to overestimate the importance of our areas of control that are always very limited and which can, thus, reinforce feelings of helplessness in us. However, we also tend to underestimate the reach of our influence. (See the section "A Story" later in this chapter.)

An exercise to try out

The sustainability inspector

This is a simple yet powerful exercise that can be done in any context or circumstance. Each student will become the *sustainability inspector* for an hour. In that capacity, they will carefully examine the objects they have in their home from a sustainability perspective and list those that are making a negative footprint, whether socially, health-wise, or environmentally.

The goal of this exercise is to help individuals notice the ways in which they are contributing to unsustainability problems. The list generally is very long, and it fills the students with surprise and horror. This exercise creates a new level of awareness, as they move from unintentional contribution to conscious awareness. And from there, they can make choices.

A story

A group of Romanian business leaders and coaches were attending a workshop in Bucharest about shaping their legacy and making a difference in the world. The conversation shifted from what impact they would like to achieve to what they felt they were able to do, and the room rapidly filled with complaints about the corruption of the system, the lack of regulatory frameworks, and unethical competitors. Rapidly, each anecdote fed upon the previous one and augmented an atmosphere of powerlessness. I invited them to pause and think of one person who had had a large, positive, but unwitting influence on who they were today. It could be a friend or a relative, or someone they never met in person—someone they just read or heard about, even someone who lived in another time.

After a few minutes of silent reflection, they all had found their person, in many cases, surprising themselves. I asked them if, in the same way, they might be influencing the lives and behaviors of people they will never meet. Every decision and every interaction create ripple effects of impact beyond our imagination.

With that insight, I asked them to think of possible actions they could take in their area of influence, if not control.

Other resources

https://sustainabledevelopment.un.org/topics/sustainabledevelop
    mentgoals The Sustainability Development Goals targets offer
    an excellent platform to create exercises. Several targets are

formulated for policymakers or governments, but many are general enough that anyone can relate to them. Students can be assigned different targets that best apply to them; they then have to identify the ways in which they are contributing to the current problems and state how they can/will modify that personal situation.

References

Antonetti, P., & Maklan, S. (2014). Feelings that make a difference: How guilt and pride convince consumers of the effectiveness of sustainable consumption choices. *Journal of Business Ethics*, *124*(1), 117–134.

Argyris, C. (1980). *Inner contradictions of rigorous research*. New York, NY: Academic Press.

Argyris, C., & Schon, D. A. (1974). *Theory in practice: Increasing professional effectiveness*. San Francisco, CA: Jossey-Bass.

Cross, R. T. (1998). Teachers' views about what to do about sustainable development. *Environmental Education Research*, *4*(1), 41–52.

Gunningham, N. (2019). Averting climate catastrophe: Environmental activism, extinction rebellion and coalitions of influence. *King's Law Journal*, *30*(2), 194–202.

Holmberg, J. (2014). Transformative learning and leadership for a sustainable future: Challenge lab at Chalmers University of Technology. In: *Intergenerational learning and transformative leadership for sustainable futures* (pp. 68–78). Wageningen, Netherlands: Wageningen Academic Publishers.

Jayaratne, M., Sullivan Mort, G., & Clare, D. S. (2015). Sustainability living in a carbon-priced economy: "Shoulds" and "woulds," making amends and sustainability guilt. *Journal of Nonprofit & Public Sector Marketing*, *27*(3), 285–306.

Kals, E., & Maes, J. (2002). Sustainable development and emotions. In: *Psychology of sustainable development* (pp. 97–122). Boston, MA: Springer.

Kühne, R. W. (2019). Climate change: The science behind Greta Thunberg and Fridays for Future.

Murray, S. (2020). Framing a climate crisis: A descriptive framing analysis of how Greta Thunberg inspired the masses to take to the streets.

O'Brien, C. (2012). Sustainable happiness and well-being: Future directions for positive psychology. *Psychology, 3*(12), 1196.

Onwezen, M. C., Bartels, J., & Antonides, G. (2014). The self-regulatory function of anticipated pride and guilt in a sustainable and healthy consumption context. *European Journal of Social Psychology, 44*(1), 53–68.

Rimanoczy, I. B. (2010). *Business leaders committing to and fostering sustainability initiatives* (Doctoral dissertation). Teachers College, Columbia University.

Sekerka, L. E., & Stimel, D. (2012). Environmental sustainability decision-making: Clearing a path to change. *Journal of Public Affairs, 12*(3), 195–205.

Starik, M. (2004). Holistic environmental leadership: Living sustainably beyond 9-to-5. *Human Ecology Review, 11*(3), 280–284.

Stir, J. (2006). Restructuring teacher education for sustainability: Student involvement through a "strengths model." *Journal of Cleaner Production, 14*(9–11), 830–836.

Swyngedouw, E. (2013). Apocalypse now! Fear and doomsday pleasures. *Capitalism Nature Socialism, 24*(1), 9–18.

Verdugo, V. C. (2012). The positive psychology of sustainability. *Environment, Development and Sustainability, 14*(5), 651–666.

Part III

Systems Thinking

The four Principles in this section belong to the content area of Systems Thinking.

Systems Thinking is a holistic approach to reality, focused on how the different parts that constitute a system are related and connected. Unlike analysis, which fragments something into its separate components, Systems Thinking looks at the patterns, flows, processes, feedback loops, and systems nested in larger systems, and how they all integrate into a whole.

Nature has been the way humans have learned Systems Thinking for millennia, by connecting causes with effects and developing resilient ways in tune with natural cycles. It may be argued that Systems Thinking is innate in humans. Nevertheless, for the past 500 years, we have distanced ourselves from Nature as a teacher and guide, confident that "rational" thinking and analytical fragmentation would provide us with all the necessary knowledge. While these processes led to formidable scientific developments, they also misled us into an anthropocentric view of life that ultimately is proving problematic. As Systems Theory researcher Russell Ackoff put it, we are alive, but no single part of our body can be alive without the whole. An automobile needs all the major parts installed and functioning properly together to be able to transport us.

When Peter Senge first promoted the understanding of systems for organizational learning, he reflected that the current state of planetary unsustainability is a manifestation of systems ignorance. He proposed that humans need to develop systems intelligence to reconnect to the innate understanding that we are capable of. Only this kind of intelligence can help humanity act in more restorative and flourishing ways.

From the different aspects that characterize Systems Thinking, I selected four dimensions that have a major role in developing a Sustainability Mindset: Long Term Thinking, Both+And Thinking, Cyclical Flow, and Interconnectedness. They are explained as Principles in this section.

4   Principle number 3

Long-term thinking

Definition

Every action has consequences that are not immediately visible. Considering the long term when analyzing situations and making decisions has a positive impact on global sustainability.

Teaching Goal

Students consider the long-term consequences and implications when analyzing situations and making decisions.

Meta Goal

To develop the habit of considering long-term impacts.

Origins of the Principle

Considering the immediate or short-term impact of a decision we are addressing comes naturally to us. The sooner the feedback information arrives, the more likely it will influence our future actions. Senge gave the example of the contaminating effect of batteries on soil when traditionally disposed of in a landfill. It proved difficult to change consumers' disposal habits because the effect is geographically distant—on an unknown landfill, then seeping into the soil and contaminating groundwater decades in the future. On the other hand, eating tainted food can rapidly sicken our body, so the short cause-and-effect cycle may help us learn to look for expiration dates on the products we consume.

Many authors have stressed that it is critical to examine the long-term effects of our decisions and behaviors, whether connected to organizations (Senge, 1990), ecology and pedagogy (Orr, 1990), altruistic behaviors (Daloz, 1996), or even to public health.[1] The focus on only the short-term effect of actions undermines complete understanding in a variety of domains. Business leaders traditionally make decisions with their focus on the quarterly report they will have to defend or on the sales or production quotas they have promised to meet. Investors look at the return on investment after only a quarter or two. Policy makers and politicians often look at likely results before their next election. Consumers make decisions based on the immediate gratification of consumption. Consequently, costs, profit, speed, efficiency, fame, or near-term feelings of success and satisfaction serve as the metrics and the goal.

Regrettably, today we are witnessing the price of eco-system damage due to cutting costs, the social burden of focusing on profit margins, and the health risks of fast-track processes. We can read in newspapers how doing things right—efficiently—does not mean we are doing the right things—effectively. In short, short-term thinking has fallen far short of making our lives better.

It is time to listen to the wisdom of indigenous peoples, who found resilient ways to exist for over 15,000 years. The "Seventh Generation Principle," recorded first in The Great Law of the Iroquois Confederacy sometime between 1142 and 1500 AD, is based on the ancient native concept that the decisions we make today should result in a sustainable world seven generations into the future. How would our decisions change if we applied this concept? How would that shape a new world?

In my research, several business leaders were explicit about how they realized that if they wanted to reduce the harm they were creating, albeit unintentionally, they had to expand their perspective about time horizons. Business as usual was causing severe problems, but they didn't know how a different way would be possible, given how their organizations were set up. They developed the growing sense that there was no choice but to go beyond the short-term mindset.

Why do we need this Principle?

Regardless of the discipline we are teaching, if we wish to have students acquire a sustainability mindset, adopting the habit of incorporating a long-term perspective will be essential to their success. Such a practice will not only allow them to reduce harm but also can enable them to solve critical problems with a broad understanding of unintended consequences—or as one systems educator put it: To be less wrong.

Certainly, it is not possible to foretell all outcomes 100 years in the future—but it is already a good first step to try to imagine them. For example, thinking beyond the current typical short-term mindset to consider the long-term, nonobvious disposal of things we purchase today may be a good start.

How is this Principle effectively brought into the classroom?

This Principle is translated into the following goals:
   Teaching Goal:

Students consider the long-term consequences and implications when analyzing situations and making decisions.

The long-term aspiration of this Principle is best stated in the **Meta Goal:**

To develop the habit of considering long-term impacts.

The context in which educators, leadership trainers, and coaches find themselves is marked by speed, demanding obligations, too little time for too many tasks to accomplish, and permanent compromises. In these circumstances, people relieve stress by acting promptly, which means making decisions with the minimum of the necessary information. This goes as much for the students as for the educators themselves.

To change this practice, one has to start developing awareness of one's personal pace and the comfortable, default habit of mind. Otherwise, we make quick decisions following the usual impulses: Instant gratification, getting things done rapidly, not giving too much thought to something by multitasking, and engaging in automatic behaviors, doing things as we have been doing them or as everybody does them. Admittedly, this behavior is common in most organizations: Acting following existing norms, policies, or standards. "Just do it" is the admired mantra that we are up against here.

Remember that the Meta Goal in this case is to develop the habit of considering long-term impacts. We are developing a new habit of the mind.

Key components

The key components in the Long-term Thinking Principle are as follows:

- Increase awareness of one's own habits related to our time perspective.
- Explore implications of a short-term perspective.
- Unleash imagination to think of possible implications in the long term.
- Heighten awareness of the short-term/long-term dilemma as seen in one's personal life.
- Connect to actions.

An essential step in acquiring a long-term perspective is to *increase awareness of one's own habits related to our time perspective.* Just to survive a busy life, we typically draw on ingrained habits with a lack of mindfulness. Unfortunately, such automatic actions often have long-term consequences we wouldn't intentionally choose. The habit of driving a mile to pick up some groceries may save a few minutes, but we may rarely consider that the carbon emissions are much greater than those from walking or biking. Buying a daily latte may feel like a great convenience until we total up the annual expenditure this represents when compared with making coffee at home.

Nothing better than a simple decision to realize the complexity of potential impacts, and how little attention we may usually pay to them. Developing this insight and how our *short-term perspective results in undesired impacts* is another key component of the Principle. How many small decisions do we make daily, absent-mindedly and automatically, that may be having long-term impacts we wouldn't intentionally choose? The COVID-19 experience is again an illuminating context to explore the unfortunate short-term thinking. For example, in some places the inconvenience of a lock-down was considered more important when making regulatory decisions than early prevention of the spread of the disease—an attitude that ultimately created more harm. This moment of awareness connects with the previous Principle of My Contribution.

We need to engage *our imagination* beyond what is obvious to *explore the implications of our behaviors in the long-term*. This is not an easy task, and it involves identifying stakeholders that may be impacted by a simple decision we take. Starting where we are may be the easiest and most powerful strategy. A student can think of a decision she is about to make that afternoon, such as whether to join a friend in planting a tree. Tree planting is a wonderful initiative, as a tree contributes to the shade of the canopy and absorbs carbon dioxide. We can benefit from more trees everywhere, so she feels great about it. Assume they will use a sprouted coconut to plant. What could possibly be long-term drawbacks from this thoughtful project? In fact, one consideration is how big this coconut tree will grow. How close will it be to the street or to the neighbors? As it produces coconuts, will they be falling on the street or on cars? Even on passersby? Who will have to trim and take care of this tree as it grows? Will there be liability issues if someone is hurt? Will the roots lift the driveway and force the homeowners to do repairs, or to remove what by then will be a large tree?

Heightening awareness of the short-term/long-term dilemma in one's personal life is important. For example, compared to the idea of planting a tree, asking to consider the long-term impacts of an immense regional project such as the Chinese dam on the Yangtze River would be more remote and less meaningful for the students. The dam will certainly cause significantly greater impact on the world than planting a coconut tree, but it is also beyond the scope of action of a student. It's practically impossible to relate to. Acquiring a shift of mindset needs to be anchored in something more personal, something deeply felt. Unless the student is personally impacted by having to abandon his home because of the flooding produced by the new dam, it won't be something personal and relevant.

Connecting to action is the payoff in absorbing a more long-term perspective in one's habit of mind. Evidence shows that habits become more embedded and unconscious as we repeatedly enact new behaviors (Duhigg, 2012). Making coffee every day may start to seem normal and, perhaps, setting a coffee maker to go on automatically in the morning may even save as much time as what we thought we gained by buying that latte.

As mentioned before, key components are leverage points that can accelerate achieving the teaching goal of a Principle, and we also must keep in mind that the Meta goal is to develop a new habit of mind. After realizing the numerous automatic decisions and behaviors we have daily, it calls for a pause to explore what the implications of our short-term habit of mind may be. This insight, which helps expand our self-awareness (see Principle Number 9) might create a number of feelings, such as the realization of our contribution, and an educator can invite students to use the fuel of emotions to move *into action*: So what is something you can or will do?

Preparing yourself for the task

We all act in numerous, automatic ways every day. It saves us energy and time and helps us get things done. Therefore, educators who want to introduce this Principle to their students should be the first ones to explore how this short-term habit of mind is present in their own lives. One simple exercise is pausing to ponder the complexity, frequency, and implications of everyday actions. It can be a powerful teaching moment to share with students about one's personal experience of challenging a short-term habit of mind and testing what it takes to expand it intentionally.

Key questions for the educator:

For self-awareness:

- Think of a current decision you are making and how introducing long-term thinking would change your decision.
- Who are the stakeholders who might be impacted by this decision?
- How far into the future can you push your imagination?
- In what decisions or daily behaviors do you recognize benefits of thinking about the long-term impacts?
- How do you feel when you give solid consideration to the long-term?
- What are some habits that you might change, and what could be a simple strategy to do so?

To prepare the assignments/activities:

- What are some examples of how short-term thinking creates unsustainable impacts?
- Where can students find further examples on their own?

Tips for the educator:

- **Prepare examples** that show the magnitude of long-term unsustainable impacts and how they are linked to decisions individuals make. It is common to assume that large impacts are made by governments, policies, and big corporations, and that individuals (like students) can only have a minimal impact. This assumption is both disempowering and untrue. It justifies cynicism and inaction. Governments and corporations don't make decisions; individuals do.
- **Take advantage of the diversity** in your audience. When imagining future scenarios, call on different disciplines that can bring new perspectives, such as the humanities, psychology, art, or literature.
- Connect this Principle with **Both+and thinking** (Principle number 4, discussed in the next chapter).
- Assign different **news media** in which students must find stories of the lack of long-term thinking.
- **Connect with action**: What can or will you do?
- When is long-term thinking not a good idea? Why? It can be powerful to foster critical thinking and to invite students to **identify exceptions**, contradicting the Principle with situations where it would not be appropriate. Exploring those circumstances can deepen greater discernment.

An exercise to try out

Before breakfast

This exercise is generic enough that it can be applied to any context.

Invite the students to list the activities they performed this morning between getting up and eating breakfast. For example, I did some stretches. I walked to the kitchen and fed the cat and cleaned its litter box. I turned on the coffeemaker. I walked to the bathroom and brushed my teeth, took a shower, washed my hair.

From that list, they then select one automatic behavior and explore the long-term impact of this behavior, be it a good impact or a not-so-good one.

Example: I buy cat food in a can. When I was a child, we had a cat at home and my grandmother used to give it whatever leftovers we had, sometimes even preparing liver for the cat. I wonder how much overfishing I am contributing to with all the pets in the developed world being fed tuna, salmon, or other ocean fish? What is the impact on the marine ecosystem of the bycatch from the industrial fisheries?

They can then share their findings and insights with a partner or in trios. With the larger group, conduct a discussion about how we are ignoring long-term impacts and what we would do if we had those in mind. The dialog can be prompted to how useful and beneficial short-term thinking is, and how we might retrain ourselves to expand the time perspective.

The goal of this exercise is to help students find the long-term impact of daily actions, notice their "long-term myopia," and realize their unintentional role. This exercise creates awareness and aims at developing a new lens to analyze decisions and behaviors.

A story

Pam, a former executive in a multinational sports and fitness corporation, relates a critical incident that shifted her thinking. It was triggered by another of several miscarriages she had, at the time that her husband was diagnosed with cancer. She had read about a drug her mother had been prescribed many decades ago to prevent her own miscarriage, with side effects that could be passed on to the mother's daughters. This medication had since been banned, but Pam was experiencing the side effects herself. In parallel, they discovered that her husband's cancer was linked to his exposure to DDT. In the past the chemical was widely used for pest control on farmlands. These two discoveries made her wonder what business decisions she and her company were making now that might have longer term consequences they had not considered to date. As a result, she began searching for the answer, asking a very different set of questions to designers and engineers, and their extended supply chain partners. Do we know or understand all the implications of our manufacturing practices, material, and design choices on the environment and health of the manufacturing workers? She ultimately played a leading role in developing a more long-term, systems perspective in the business, starting in the product design area and infiltrating the whole organization.[2]

Other resources

Short termism and long-term thinking in corporations by Tima Bansal. https://www.youtube.com/watch?v=Ti70jUHhz_c

Short termism in all our acts of our life: Change your mindset, TED Talk by Futurist Ari Wallach. https://www.youtube.com/watch?v=J-8fYhwrYzI

Long Term thinking to build resilience in Water sustainability. Values shift. National Science Federation video. https://www.youtube.com/watch?v=tfvMTFCw5Is

Cartoon video on short-term plans and long-term goals (also for the Principle Both/And). https://www.youtube.com/watch?v=De0HyiqRXIU

Summit 2017 Long-term strategy in a short term world—Corporate perspectives. https://www.youtube.com/watch?v=jN4dOT55utg

Short and long term thinking in wine making industry—Arpad Molnar video. https://www.youtube.com/watch?v=yZTfmhCjBRI

Video of Peter Senge at Aalto University, Finland. Being better in
the world of systems. http://sal30.aalto.fi
https://www.youtube.com/watch?v=vp8v2Udd_PM

Notes

1. See Value of Systems Thinking—US Center for Disease Control: https://www.youtube.com/watch?v=Fo3ndxVOZEo.
2. Rimanoczy, I. (2013). *Big Bang Being: Developing the Sustainability Mindset*. Routledge Taylor & Francis Group. p. 10.

References

Daloz, L. A. (1996). *Common fire: Lives of commitment in a complex
world*. Boston, MA: Beacon Press.

Duhigg, C. (2012). *The power of habits: Why we do what we do in life
and business*. New York, NY: Random House.

Orr, D. W. (1990). Environmental education and ecological literacy.
The Education Digest, 55(9), 49.

Senge, P. (1990). *The fifth discipline: The art and practice of organizational
learning*. New York, NY: Doubleday.

5 Principle number 4
Both+and thinking

Definition
Both+and thinking allows us to understand paradoxes and calls for creative solutions that are inclusive of all stakeholders.
Teaching Goal
Students recognize either/or solutions, understand their limitations, and practice both+and thinking to accept paradoxes and create inclusive solutions.
Meta Goal
To develop the habit of seeing the "either/or" factor at play and intentionally promote both+and thinking.

Origins of the Principle

Some years ago I was meeting with the dean of a business school in Shanghai. I had just finished a presentation about research on the Sustainability Mindset for a group of faculty, when he approached me with an apologetic smile, saying "Very interesting, but you know, here in China we have much to do to catch up with the Western world. We cannot focus on sustainability, we have to focus on business." His statement caught me by surprise and I reflected for a long time on how I should have responded. Only afterward did I think of a possible question: How do you carry out business without a planet?

I am certain that the dean would react differently today, with all the information available and the social pressure to address the sustainability challenges of our planet (or our city). This is, however, not unlike a statement we all have heard too often: "Make a choice: either business or planet." Do we really have a choice?

Sustainability beliefs aside, either-or statements are very common: Either for Brexit or against it; either pro-migrants or against; either focus on profit or on people; either business or nonprofit; either quality or speed; either my political party or yours. And, they can be dramatic too, as when doctors had to decide which patients would receive available ventilators during the COVID-19 crisis, and which ones would be left to die. There may be no solution to accommodate a both+and thinking. It may turn out to be so in certain situations. Some dilemmas need a decision that excludes the other option, like when we choose to buy one car or the other. Other dilemmas are ongoing, and in fact they are not problems to be solved, but are polarities that are interconnected, and need to be managed (Johnson, 1992). However, we are more used to approach every situation with either/or thinking.

Much of the dualistic thinking over the centuries has arisen from the predominance of rational thinking and logic, which operate under the either/or logic (McGilchrist, op.cit.). However, this means of processing information has proven not to be absolute. Eastern philosophies and religions have called for an integration of dualities (Tsao & Laszlo, op.cit.). Aboriginal and native traditions are anchored in the complementarity of forces, such as day and night, moon and sun, animal and human souls.

Eisler (1987) proposed a socio-anthropological perspective, studying the origins and expressions of the "dominator model," where one faction seeks to dominate and impose its worldview or truth to the exclusion of other views. This "superiority" can be observed throughout history to the present in a multitude of ways: in religions, class systems, and ethnic or racial contexts; in the frameworks of gender and professional employment; in the Western world with respect to developing countries, to name a few. Eisler proposes a partnership model, where diversity can coexist and thrive. The partnership model is one where individuals can be valued by the contributions they bring, rather than by the superiority/inferiority hierarchy that marks the domination models.

Developmental psychologists over the past four decades have tended to address the either/or approach by connecting it with the personal developmental stages expressed in every person's worldview. This approach brought a whole new depth of insight into the either/or and both+and logic. As we develop, we go through stages with a progressively broader scope of caring, that is to say, from ego-centric to socio-centric to world-centric (Cook-Greuter, 2002, 2005). Starting with birth, we journey from a focus on "what I need" (survival mode) at the expense of all others, to caring for a few (the tribe), to more and more inclusive perspectives, eventually reaching levels of oneness with all that is. Kohlberg (1958) described stages of moral development, from pre-conventional to conventional and post-conventional, with an increasing interest in and appreciation of others. Jane Loevinger (1976) described nine sequential stages of ego development, each one more complex than the previous one in how individuals perceive themselves in relation to the world. Every stage provides a frame of reference that organizes received information and integrates that information in a model of "including and transcending."

In a similar way, Graves (1974) identified eight levels, which he called "tiers," of human value systems of increasing complexity with differentiated worldviews, purposes, and preferences. For example, the first tier is characterized by a narrow subsistence-level perspective; this first tier evolves to a second tier with more inclusive perspectives and so forth. Beck and Cowan (1996) based their Spiral Dynamics model of development on Graves' work, defining colors for eight phases of evolution in our adaptive intelligence. The model starts with the color beige for the instinctive self-focus on survival, then moving through increasingly less self-centered levels up to the seventh level (yellow) representing the integral self, and the eighth level (turquoise) for the holistic self. Kegan described the developmental evolution of consciousness in terms of "orders of making meaning," where individuals move from a first order (impulsive) to a second (instrumental), to a third (socialized), to the fourth (self-authoring), and to the fifth order (self-transforming mind). Barrett Brown (2006) prepared a comparison of several different developmental stage models—from Graves, Beck and Cowan, Loevinger, Cook-Greuter, Piaget, Wilber, and Aurobindo—organizing them into 14 colored zones encompassing egocentric, ethnocentric, world centric, and cosmocentric stages.

What these different models have in common is the increasing complexity in how we see ourselves, what we identify with, what we are aware of, what our value systems are—in sum, what we care about. They also describe increasing levels of inclusion of other people and of different inputs, which is a very important aspect in the development of a Sustainability Mindset. Do we accept that others are different, think differently, have differing needs and paradigms, or do we choose to neglect and ignore them as we make decisions? Stakeholder inclusion correlates with social sensitivity. Including others who are different, and refraining from "converting or convincing them," is an expression of the both+and thinking and has a direct impact in shaping a world that works for all.

The evolution is neither inevitable nor equal for every individual, and our personal experiences and introspection or contemplative practices can move us along the continuum. Each stage has its characteristics and provides a particular lens through which we make meaning out of the world. Depending on what stage of development mostly shapes our worldview, we may see others as instruments for the satisfaction of our needs (earlier stage); see enemies that threaten our safety or identity (following stage); distinguish "our people" from strangers who can endanger our family or nation; see commonalities with others even though they seem different; or, at the higher levels, see what we share with all living beings. These different lenses, which we automatically use, drive our reactions, feelings, and behaviors, and while we may move from one stage to the next, we "include and transcend" all the previous ones. Like the reptilian brain that is present in our heads, so too are all our previous lenses still present, dormant but present. In a given situation, let's say a dark back street, we may revert to the survivalist mode (it's either you or me), perhaps only to reflect that, in fact, we are not in danger and can replace our defensive posture with positive curiosity about a stranger walking toward us (I will be careful, but retain an open mind).

Why do we need this Principle?

After mulling the different stages of consciousness proposed by developmental psychologists, how do we connect this perspective back to the either/or and both+and logic, particularly when processing information about our planet? This is precisely where the richness of the Principle comes into play. The Principle invites us to intentionally aim at noticing the either/or logic and realizing its consequences and impacts; it also prompts us to consider the consequences and impacts of using both+and logic. In a simple way, the Principle can guide educators and students to expand their consciousness.

With the examples of either/or thinking mentioned above, it becomes clear that when decisions are made solely from that perspective, they tend to exclude the opinion of key stakeholders, prioritizing one opinion over the other and creating zero-sum solutions. I win, you lose. You win, I lose.

We don't have to look too far to realize the complicated consequences of this perspective in today's world. For example, some feel that we face environmental challenges because profit is seen as being jeopardized if we take care of environmental conditions. We prioritize profit, but then the environmental impacts come back and haunt us in very concrete ways. For example, increased consumption of furniture stimulates increased logging of forests → which releases the CO_2 stored in the trees into the atmosphere → and also eliminates the trees necessary to absorb future CO_2 → which changes weather patterns → which creates droughts or floods → which may force us to move out of our homes and abandon the nice new furniture. One can use this example of "chain-linked possibilities" with a variety of situations: social challenges, health-related concerns, peace efforts, etc. Clearly, these are not problems to be solved, but ongoing polarities that have to be managed.

In my research (Rimanoczy, 2010, op.cit.), it became clear that the business leaders I studied had understood the limitations and inadequacy of their either/or "business as usual" perspective and felt confronted by the challenge of creating solutions and processes that would consider the needs of a wider scope of stakeholders—for example, the employees of outsourced manufacturing sites in Asia or the next generations (See Story section in this chapter).

These leaders realized that either/or logic rarely leads to effective solutions, particularly if it is based on a win/lose perspective. On the other hand, when we approach a situation with the both+and logic, we use an inclusive perspective that can open new possibilities.

It definitely requires creativity to invent new options that are inclusive, but the results justify the effort. These types of solutions are key to the health of the ecosystem and they can create fair and peaceful societies. As an example, here are some areas where either/or solutions can result in further, new problems and, therefore, require solutions that could benefit from a both+and approach/thinking:

- Interpersonal conflict
- Intergenerational conflicts
- Relationships among political parties
- Neighborhood/community issues
- Racial and ethnic coexistence
- Religious coexistence
- Peace negotiations
- Trade agreements
- Business decisions
- Stakeholder considerations
- Environmental protection
- Public health challenges
- Union negotiations
- Policy making
- Immigration policies
- Budget allocations
- Sustainable development
- Urban planning
- Technology development and AI

How is this Principle introduced into the classroom?

This Principle is translated into the following **Teaching Goal:**

> *Students recognize either/or solutions, explore the limitations, and practice both+and thinking to accept paradoxes and create inclusive solutions.*

The long-term aspiration of this Principle is best stated in the **Meta Goal:**

*To develop the habit of seeing the "either/or" factor in action
and intentionally promote both+and thinking.*

We are entering here again in the domain of automatic
habits of mind, particularly automatic ways of processing information. Without giving it extensive thought,
we weigh only two options in making a decision: "either
this or that." This tendency is pervasive in our daily lives,
and we find it very useful since it aids us to move swiftly
through the day. Imagine having to slowly ponder whether
to take the car or walk, whether to order appetizers or not,
whether to dress casual or a bit more formal—and then
look for complicated "both+and" solutions. These simple
examples should make the point.

The problem arises if dualistic thinking is the default
way we face the world. By being used to quickly making
hundreds of small choices throughout the day, we may not
even pause to check if the same logic is the best tool for the
occasion. As with any habit, the first step is to realize *we
have* a habit and that it may be at the root of some unwanted
consequences. The next step is to realize there are alternative approaches , such as the both+and perspective.

The Meta Goal will be to develop the students' alert-
ness to first notice the "either/or" logic at play in different
situations, particularly those that are problematic (or can
become so), and then when to use the more appropriate
both+and tool. Perhaps by doing this, we may prompt
individuals in their developmental journey as they move
toward stages where the scope for caring is expanded.

Key components

The key components in this Principle are as follows:

- Distinguishing between problems to solve and polarities to manage
- Paradox – Ambiguity

- Complexity – Uncertainty
- Inclusion
- Stakeholders
- Links of the either/or logic to fundamentalism.

The first objection that we may come across when suggesting a both+and possibility will be the *paradox*. I have heard the paradox argument often:

> *But how can we possibly make money AND spend more on environmental practices?*
>
> *How can we possibly be true to our values (our constituents, our shareholders, our friends, the law) AND accept/tolerate those who contradict the very essence of our principles?*

As mentioned before, the first step is to help distinguish between problems that need to be solved because there is something that can make them disappear, and tensions between polarities that have to be managed, because they represent two poles that are interconnected. Polarities represent a continuous situation, for example the tension between autonomy and interdependence (Johnson, op.cit). The educator can provide some examples, and ask students to find some other examples on their own, to practice this new distinction.

We are so trained to stand for what we value with courage and advocacy that we may find it difficult to even imagine living the *paradox* of both+and. It may bring up feelings of disloyalty; feelings of cowardice as we fail to defend our opinions and beliefs; fears of letting down our tribe; or loss of self-respect. This may even reach to the core of who we are. We ARE our values, we don't just have them; our principles and beliefs ARE our identity.

It may be appropriate for the educator to facilitate a dialog where these concerns can be expressed, without the need for "correcting" them. Using the perspective offered by developmental psychologists, we see that each individual is looking through the personal prism of their developmental stage. The concerns should not be viewed as right or wrong; they are just real and different ways of making meaning. At the same time, listening to others share their perspectives (without seeking to convince anyone and reach a unified conclusion) can be a powerful stimulus for opening new ways of seeing a situation.

Asking students to identify other paradoxes in their lives may also be helpful as a way for them to become more comfortable with the whole notion of paradoxes. There will be no shortage of examples. Stories and anecdotes from the students' daily lives may surface their own resources for dealing with *ambiguity* and the creative solutions they may have found. The exercise can serve to remind them of their past experience with the both+and option and the solutions this option offered.

A conversation like this will bring up the challenge of *uncertainty*, since we may not have sufficient information (or ideas) to create a both+and solution. In a way, we will be developing the system intelligence of the students, as we point out the *complexity* of reality and the uncertainty that is a characteristic of our time. The audience might be familiar with the expression that we are living in the time of VUCA: volatility, uncertainty, complexity, and ambiguity. Again, this may elicit feelings of fear or anxiety, particularly if we have a strong need to be in control, to know all the answers, to demonstrate our smartness to impress others—and ourselves. As with all Principles, we are developing the Sustainability Mindset, and this corresponds to the interior dimension of the individual.

An additional component, that of *inclusion*, is equally important to this Principle. The very phrase "both+and" suggests inclusion of diverse parts or participants. In any discipline, we will face situations where inclusion will increase engagement and facilitate implementation of ideas, just as the exclusion of new ideas and participation by other persons will cause obstacles and hurdles. Related to this is the widely studied, and important, element of *stakeholder* input and influence (Freeman, 2010).

Traditionally, in both business and society, the focus has been on identifying and responding to the rights of shareholders, but more recent decision-making processes have been notable for their broader consideration of all those who will be impacted by a decision. These processes extend to including input into the decision by any impacted person or party interested in the decision, which might include the importance of considering the possible perspectives of stakeholders from the next generations and how Nature is a stakeholder itself.

Finally, the either/or logic can be explored from the perspective of a *fundamentalist* approach, which typically holds only one truth as the valid one. How is the belief that there is a right/wrong duality, that one truth exists to the exclusion and negation of all other truths, conditioning fundamentalist behaviors? Whether it is racial, religious, ethnical, political, or philosophical, either/or logic may be in evidence in many socially exclusionary movements. The work of Riane Eisler, through her Ted Talks and writings, can provide food for thought and discussion.

Preparing yourself for the task

As was the case in the previous Principles, educators will benefit from taking the time to explore their own habits, their own beliefs, their own preferences, in order to expand their personal awareness and, thus, be better prepared to facilitate conversations with the students.

What follows are a few questions that may help in exploring the both+and logic in our own lives.

Key questions for the educator:

For greater self-awareness:

- What makes the either/or the appropriate, or the only, way to deal with issues? Why is this so?

- How might a coach or a mentor respond to your reply?
- How do you personally feel about ambiguity and uncertainty?
- How do you deal with ambiguous challenges to which you simply don't have a clear solution?
- How comfortable are you with accepting a both+and approach to solving a challenge?
- What has been a situation where you have tried to use a both+and approach? How did it go?
- What did you learn about yourself?

To prepare the assignments/activities:

- What is a current challenging situation in which you find yourself? (You will decide how much you want to share it with the group, but it will be helpful to identify your own feelings and insights.)
- In what situations can both+and be inappropriate?
- How can the both+and approach be connected with the developmental goal of "including and transcending"?

Tips for the educator:

- Find and have ready some examples of paradoxes.
- Examples in the media abound. The more personal the examples (from the life of the student, not public ones), the higher the impact.
- Find ways to connect to the COVID-19 crisis. For example, the lack of ventilators created painful either/or choices for doctors who had to decide whom to keep alive and whom they had to let die. This prompted car manufacturers Ford, General Motors, and Tesla to consider starting to produce ventilators and other urgently needed health equipment. How can this be analyzed?
- Consider the "include and transcend" option and find an example to illustrate this.

• Remember that people will have feelings about this
  Principle: Uncertainty can be exciting for some and a
  serious stressor for others. Acknowledging and naming
  feelings may help.

An exercise to try out

The either/or detector

This is an exercise in five steps that can be done individually as an assignment or individually in class and for group
discussion or sharing.

> Step 1. Invite the students to identify a current
> decision they have to make or that they have
> recently made. It doesn't matter how important
> that decision is. Write down the decision and
> the context.
> Step 2. Ask them to use the Either/Or Detector lens
> in the decision they wrote down and analyze if
> that was the logic, or if they used both+and logic,
> or part of it.
> Step 3. What was or what might be the impact? Ask
> them to list the possible impacts of using that logic.
> Step 4. What could they do differently? Invite them
> to write down their reflections.
> Step 5. Ask them to write down a list of situations
> where they used the both+and logic.

Students may share their thoughts in pairs or trios, or in
the large group.

The goal of this exercise is to practice noticing what logic
we are using, observing the impacts and consequences, and
practicing a different, more inclusive approach. It also helps
explore feelings around uncertainty, control, complexity,
paradoxes, and conflict, and can be a practice for creative
thinking.

A story

Pam, the executive mentioned in the last chapter, returned from a product development trip to Asia convinced that her organization had to change its manufacturing practices. She had asked a pregnant woman who was working on the assembly line whether or not the smell of the adhesive (volatile organic compounds or VOC's) used to bond parts of the sports shoes together bothered her. Her answer caused her to meet directly with the head of Product Chemistry to see if there were alternatives to this compound that did not have the negative environmental and health impacts of what had been used in the industry for decades. This began a four-year process of research and testing, and ultimately substituting the use of VOC's for a completely nontoxic, water-based solvent. However, for the solution to be 100% effective, this new chemistry had to be shared with all of their competitors because of the shared manufacturing facilities. This had never been done and was a huge corporate decision that needed to be made. Ultimately, the decision was made to share this advancement at no cost to their competitors but for the health of all, opening the way for more collaboration.

However, it wasn't just a simple "substitution" process. It forced the design, materials, and development teams to begin experimenting with other "design for environment" principles, which included significantly reducing or eliminating waste, designing for disassembly and recycling, reducing the carbon footprint (through material choices and manufacturing processes), and many more actions. All of this required the product teams to step away from the traditional "either/or" thinking: Either we gain the competitive advantage or we share it with competitors; either we design a non-harmful component or we are cost-efficient. The challenges called for new both+and solutions that would aim at the financial bottom line and also at the greater good.

One of the key learnings during this time was that the teams in the organization needed to consider the whole "system" of the product design and value chain (understanding of Interconnectedness, Principle number 6) to address the economic impacts of their decisions as well as the environmental impact. It required creative innovation (Principle number 7, what is it we want to create) versus a problem-solving orientation, which does not take a systems perspective. The company became a leader in innovating the design of responsibly manufactured sporting shoes. A Sustainability Mindset in action.

Other resources

Video about what we have in common – inclusion. https://www.youtube.com/watch?v=jD8tjhVO1Tc

TED Talk about either/or and both+and. https://www.youtube.com/watch?v=3uLHjwpuFXc

Short (3 min) video from the Conscious Leadership Academy/ University San Diego about either/or and both+and in our polarized world. https://www.youtube.com/watch?v=oi1nq_sVt_E

References

Beck, D. E. & Cowan, C. (1996). *Spiral dynamics: Mastering values, leadership, and change.* Oxford, UK: Blackwell Publishing.

Brown, B. (2006). An overview of developmental stages of consciousness, Integral Institute, April 3, 2006. Retrieved from: https://integralwithoutborders.net/sites/default/files/resources/Overview%20of%20Developmental%20Levels.pdf. Accessed February 7, 2020.

Cook-Greuter, S. (2002). A detailed description of the development of nine action logics in the leadership development framework: Adapted from ego development theory. Retrieved from http://www.harthillusa.com/Detailed%20descrip.%20of%20ego%20develop%20stages.pdf

Cook-Greuter, S. (2005). Making the case for a developmental perspective. Retrieved from http://www.harthill.co.uk/publications.htm

Eisler, R. T. (1987). *The chalice and the blade*. London: Thorsons Publishing House.

Freeman, R. E. (2010). *Strategic management: A stakeholder approach*. Cambridge, UK: Cambridge University Press.

Graves, C. (1974). Human nature prepares for a momentous leap. *The Futurist, 8*(2), 72–87.

Johnson, B. (1992). Polarity management: Identifying and managing unsolvable problems. *Human resource development*. Amherst, MA: HRD Press.

Kegan, R. (1982). *The evolving self: Problem and process in human development*. Cambridge, MA: Harvard University Press.

Kohlberg, L. (1958). *The development of modes of thinking and choices in Years 10 to 16* (Ph.D. Dissertation). University of Chicago, Chicago, IL.

Loevinger, J. (1976). *Ego development: Conceptions and theories*. San Francisco, CA: Jossey-Bass.

6 Principle number 5

Flow in cycles

Definition

There are no linear processes in Nature: Everything flows in cycles of birth, growth, death, and rebirth. Many aspects of man-made unsustainability of the planet are a result of the misconception that we are not governed by this law of Nature.

Teaching Goal

Students identify how losing sight of the law of natural cycles has created unsustainability.

Meta Goal

To develop the cognitive habit of seeking the larger cycles.

Origins of the Principle

The late Ray Anderson founded the pioneering sustainability carpet company Interface, Inc. He once observed that the biggest culprit in planetary decline is the industrial system that takes resources from the Earth and makes objects that end up as waste in landfills or incinerators in a take-make-waste system. He realized that this linear way of thinking was at odds with how Nature operates. For an industry leader himself, this awareness made a profound impact on Anderson's life, prompting him to engage his leadership team and employees in radically transforming the company. The paramount changes needed were symbolized in the image of his vision: We have to climb Mount Sustainability!

The systemic Principle of Flow in Cycles connects two concepts from biological sciences. Flow is defined as matter and energy moving with unbroken continuity into and out of a system. Cycle is something that repeats itself regularly. Astronomers, physicists, biologists, and archeologists are accustomed to looking at wide time frames to identify patterns of flows and cycles. However, this thought practice is not common in other professions or in our daily endeavors. This longer timespan is similar to that in the Long-Term Thinking Principle. When we focus our attention on a shorter time span, there is much that we may be missing about multicauses and multieffects and about the eventual consequences of our decisions.

The business practices and associated consumer behaviors we exhibit in short timeframes make us inattentive to the impacts of the linear take-make-waste practice that Anderson denounced. Nature is misunderstood as an infinite resource, something to use and which can't possibly be exhausted. Traveling through miles of desert or forested mountain ranges anywhere on the globe can give us the erroneous impression that nothing we do could possibly damage such a large planetary ecosystem, but that is simply human myopia. We must recognize the relatively new phenomenon of "desertification" where there was no desert before, and the huge expanses of cut-down and incinerated old-growth forests.

Similarly, the disposal of products and materials has been given little attention over the centuries. In the past, when consumption was at low levels, the disposal of organic matter was merely returned to the Earth. With the beginning of the Industrial Revolution, the volume of manufactured goods increased, making many new products available to larger populations. This improved our comfort and standard of living, while the step of disposal remained unseen. But, when we throw something away, where does it actually go? Enlightened citizens today have to concede that what we dispose of doesn't just disappear; it is just relocated to another place. We need to expand our consciousness about the impact of consumption and the role everyone is playing in this problem (see the Story at the end of this chapter).

Part of the systemic ignorance of life cycles is reflected in the cultural denial of aging and death in many Northern and Western cultures. Plastic surgery, fitness programs, fad diets, cosmetics, and brain exercises invite us to defy aging. While many Eastern cultures honor their elders, parts of the world widely value youth and ignore irresistible biological processes, signifying the belief that humans are somehow beyond the laws of Nature. In similar ways, the organizations we establish subscribe to the same myth: Problems are analyzed seeking linear cause-and-effect connections and strategies and metrics call for endless incremental growth. The idea of infinite growth, however, is an economic construct that defies the laws of Nature. A business may look like shares, paper trails, processes, services, or even intangibles, yet nothing humans do is outside of Nature.

For example, climate warming compounded with fertilizer runoff has created over 400 hypoxic (oxygen-depleted) dead zones in our oceans, lakes, and ponds, where no marine life can survive. A study from the University of California found that the recovery period of dead zones can last 1,000 years (Moffitt, Hill, Roopnarine, & Kennett, 2015). Overfishing, loss of rainforests due to industrial farming or logging, loss of soil due to industrial agriculture practices, and loss of community due to urban sprawl are just some other examples of the impact of linear growth models. More recently, during the COVID-19 lockdown in Italy, the interruption of cruise lines navigating the canals of Venice prompted the fish to come back and led to cleaner waters. What this, in fact, showed us was that the linear growth of tourism does have a damaging impact on the ecosystems. It may seem ok for the pleasure of travelers and the economy, but it is not without a cost, and there are many other consequences that are less visible than the disappearance of the fish.

Interestingly, while the assumption that growth can be infinite has been denounced by some scholars for decades (Drucker, 1994; Kassel, 2013; Meadows, Meadows, Randers, & Behrens, 1972), it has persisted as a shared assumption held by business leaders, entrepreneurs, and politicians. Introduced at an academic conference in Paris in 2008, a movement called "de-growth" or "post-growth" has emerged, calling for the revision of a paradigm dating to the Industrial Revolution (Blühdorn, 2017; Demaria, Schneider, Sekulova, & Martinez-Alier, 2013; Kallis, 2011; Martinez-Alier, 2012). This movement questions the traditional measurement of well-being through the GDP, which includes all goods sold during a 12-month period. Few people recognize that GDP includes sales of stolen goods, recovery expenditures from natural disasters, public health spending and drug-related expenses, weapons and war equipment, and other things that cannot be connected to the highest levels of human well-being. At the same time, the GDP excludes items such as unpaid voluntary services, childcare by parents staying home, and neighbors and relatives taking care of elderly people, all of which can be essential to a community's prosperity and happiness.

Other approaches addressing the unwanted consequences of our economic paradigm have been developed through models that consider the life cycle of products in a circular way. Early sustainability advocates promoted a "Cradle to Grave" outlook for industrial design, where companies should consider the processes of production, distribution, transportation, and user disposal of their products to minimize landfills and incineration. More recently, theorists have urged a "circular economy," coining the term "Cradle to Cradle." This thinking calls for businesses to plan on how post-use products can be creatively repurposed. This is different from the traditional scope of the manufacturer's responsibility, which ends with the consumer using the product and doesn't care when, where, and how it will be disposed of afterward (Bocken, De Pauw, Bakker, & van der Grinten, 2016; George, Lin, & Chen, 2015; Kirchherr, Reike, & Hekkert, 2017; McDonough & Braungart, 2010).

Part of this approach is "upcycling," where discarded products can be not just recycled but become components of new products, thus neither disposing (down-cycling) nor recycling but rather up-cycling them, as in an "upgrade" (Ahn & Lee, 2018; McDonough & Braungart, 2013; Sung & Sung, 2015; Wilson, 2016).

The cyclical nature of all ecological processes is an important Principle of ecology. Ecosystems generate feedback loops where nutrients are continually recycled. All organisms produce waste, but waste for one species is food for another. Therefore, there is no such thing as "waste" in Nature. The Earth's ecosystem has evolved in this way over four billion years, using and recycling the same matter: Minerals, water, air (Capra & Luisi, 2014). However, without much thought, now we are releasing into the biosphere thousands of synthetic chemical compounds, plastics, and metal alloys that cannot be broken down by Nature. We are disrupting natural cycles and modifying the ecological balance of water, air, and soil (Laszlo, 1989). With the anthropocentric arrogance of having invented machines, we assume we can also invent and improve Nature, while not necessarily learning from the four billion years of knowledge. Biologist Janine Benyus (1997) observed this phenomenon and proceeded to develop the concept of Biomimicry, pointing at how we can find answers and solutions to the design of products by studying how Nature has resolved similar challenges.

There has been recent attention paid to aboriginal and indigenous wisdom, inviting us to learn from knowledge developed and transmitted over millennia about successful adaptation and resilience (Beckford, Jacobs, Williams, & Nahdee, 2010; Burns, 2015; Hendry, 2014; Santha, Fraunholz, & Unnithan, 2010). Sustainable communities operating under a paradigm of harmony with others and with Nature have also provided important insights. Helena Norberg-Hodge studied the community of Ladakh in the 1970s in the northern region of India. This ancient community had efficiently adapted to extremely hard winters. During the milder seasons, they organized the necessary work according to the skills and physical aptitudes of the members. With the onset of cold weather, they had provisions guaranteeing their subsistence and made music, sang, and enjoyed other social activities. Norberg-Hodge reflects in her book and movie what a different model of well-being may look like (Norberg-Hodge, 2009). The Colombian community of Gaviotas constitutes a more contemporary experiment with alternative models (Weisman, 2008). These sources of ancestral wisdom prompt us to question "enoughness," and make us ponder in what ways we have come to equate consumption with the illusionary pursuit of happiness. Economics Professor Clair Brown proposes a new economic model built upon equality, sustainability, and right living. Brown builds on the work of Jeffrey Sachs, focused on economic development and poverty; on environmentalist Bill McKibben; and on Buddhism to line out a new economic paradigm. She links interdependence, shared prosperity, equity, sustainability, and compassion to envision a different way of living, less centered on consumption and more meaningful (Brown, 2017)—something in line with the concept of "plenitude" developed by economist Juliet Schor (2010). Laszlo Zsolnai, from Corvinus University in Hungary, has opened the perspective of a "post materialistic" business, pointing to economics as a moral science. Connecting ethics, business, and spiritual traditions, Zsolnai reflects that we need a caring management with a new ethos that takes into account society, future generations, and Nature, while serving the financial purposes of the business and the wider community (O'Higgins & Zsolnai, 2017; Setter & Zsolnai, 2019; Zsolnai, 2015). If, on the contrary, we design organizations and systems that go against the ecological principles of the Earth, as when we design linear systems of infinite growth while Nature operates in cycles, we experience the feedback and readjustments that the natural system provides. This is happening right now.

Why do we need this Principle?

Developing a systems view to analyze information and make decisions, particularly through the understanding of the cyclical flow that governs all Nature (humans and our activities included), has broad implications. As we can see in the section above, it touches how we see ourselves in relation to the cycles of growth, development, and aging.

- It impacts our sense of identity and challenges traditional behavior and consumption decisions to strive to be forever young, active, healthy, and attractive.
- It impacts industrial practices, with linear growth models, and through this the increased use of natural resources to the point of depletion or extinction.
- The flow in cycles contradicts the linear growth assumed by many politicians, which can contribute to just feeling resigned to a perpetual inability to serve the most vulnerable, versus an aspiration to change the status quo.

This broad spectrum of implications of a linear way of thinking can be touched and influenced by developing in individuals the capacity to identify linear models of thinking when they see them and to practice applying a cyclical flow approach to their own thinking and decision making.

How is this Principle effectively brought into the classroom?

This Principle is translated into the following Goals:

>**Teaching Goal:** *Students identify how losing sight of the law of Natural cycles has created unsustainability.*

>**Meta Goal:**

>*To develop the cognitive habit of seeking the natural cycles and impacts when analyzing data and making decisions.*

The previous section presented a partial list of social and environmental impacts caused by the linear ways of thinking, whether by individuals, organizations, or governments. It provides a glimpse into the breadth of the unseen impact of a way of thinking that is mostly unconscious and automatic. It also demonstrates the significant potential leverage of addressing habits of mind—the thinking patterns of students and leaders.

In contrast with its potentially large impact, the teaching goal is simple: To connect the law of natural cycles with human behavior and to identify how artificial linear thinking is a root cause of our unsustainability. Establishing this connection offers a powerful way to expand consciousness and develop new thinking patterns. This is the educator's meta-goal: To ultimately develop new systemic habits of processing information, so that the students can apply this new lens to their work or personal decision making, asking themselves the question: Am I being a linear thinker here? What are the cycles that I am missing?

Key components

The key components in this Principle are as follows:

* *Cycles in Nature: What biology and four billion years teaches us*
* *Economic Linear growth models*

- *Consumption and Identity*
- *Nature as a resource for the take-make-waste system*

These key components may be covered in the class-room in different sequences depending on the subject being taught. Since *cycles in Nature* form the foundation of this Principle, biology can best teach us what flowing in cycles means and how prevalent it is, whether occurring in days or over centuries. This may be an appropriate starting point to inquire how this Law of Nature is found in our everyday life and how it is typically absent in the way we decide, produce, and consume.

Introducing traditional *economic growth models*, with the historical perspective of the Industrial Revolution, can provide a framework for understanding where the para-digm of linear growth originated. When developing a Sustainability Mindset, we are uncovering different angles of a shared paradigm that shapes us, even while mostly invisible. This discovery may allow students to establish connections between unintentional linear thinking pat-terns and unsustainable consequences. Nothing seemed to be wrong with wanting a more comfortable life, providing increasing returns to shareholders who provide their capi-tal to others—until the impacts became visible.

People in developed societies commonly experience a link between their consumption and their *personal identity*—what makes them who they are and what values they iden-tify with. Increasing students' awareness of that link can represent a powerful pedagogical strategy. It can help them identify the purchases they make to enhance their identity and to what media messages they are most sensitive. This, in turn, can help surface their personal linear way of think-ing, with instant gratification, the denial of aging or death, and the myth of infinite growth.

Our consumption is the fuel of industrial practices: How are we part of the *take-make-waste system*? This connects us back to Principle Number 2, Our Contribution. While a reaction of dismay arises at first, this realization can actually serve as the cornerstone of our empowerment. For example, Annie Leonard's series of videos around The Story of Stuff are simple yet thought-provoking presentations of the different ways we are part of the take-make-waste system.

Preparing yourself for the task

Key questions for the educator:

For self-awareness:

- In what aspects of my life do I think in linear terms, not acknowledging the cycles of life?
- How would that realization change my attitudes? My feelings?
- How do I personally feel about infinite growth? Does my lifestyle reflect this paradigm in some ways? How?

To prepare the assignments and activities:

- How does this Principle connect with the discipline I am teaching? Establish those connections first before seeking activities.
- What could be some good videos or readings relevant both to the course and to this Principle?
- What are the benefits of the linear way of thinking?

Tips for the educator:

- Students with a background in natural sciences or biology can provide valuable input, since this Principle may be a familiar way of thinking for them.
- Biomimicry is a domain that can spark inspiring links between industrial design and the laws of Nature.
- The COVID-19 crisis has interesting aspects to explore, for example, the linear growth of tourism, and its impact on the ecosystem.

- Good examples can be found in the Ancestral wisdom of different traditions and in indigenous wisdom: Why did native tribes survive for thousands of years? How much is enough?
- There are many valuable new models to show this Principle in action: Biomimicry designs, Circular Economy initiatives, Natural Capitalism, Cradle to Cradle, the video The Story of Solutions, and Upcycling innovations. However, if the educator starts with these solutions before exploring the deeper aspects of the paradigm, the conversation will remain at a superficial, cognitive level, and not reach the transformative depth of the personal implications. It is important to remember that we are dealing with principles that can serve as leverage for a shift in the mindset, which is something personal and internal to the individual. The power rests not in the intellectual understanding, but in the experiential, deep-felt insights, in the "AHA! moments" of the student when it becomes personal. Thus, the recommendation is to refrain from quickly jumping to solutions and to introduce these only after students have sufficiently explored their personal meaning and values in this context.

An exercise to try out

Two Research Exercises and a So-What Statement

1 **Biomimicry:** Invite students to explore Biomimicry through the site https://biomimicry.org/ and select one example of a product design inspired by Nature. Have them list all the characteristics that made this product in tune with Nature, through cyclical flow and other Principles if appropriate. Invite them also to critique if the application meets sustainability criteria, or if not, what is lacking.

This is an experiential and self-directed learning exercise. The goal of this exercise is to gain a new understanding of the wisdom of Nature (the result of four billion years of trial and learning). They should discover how that knowledge is currently being applied by innovative companies to solve design challenges so as to open their thinking to new ways of producing and consuming more sustainably.

2 **Extinct Companies:** Ask students to research a company that has gone out of business and analyze to what extent linear thinking may have been a cause of its demise.

This is also an experiential, self-directed learning exercise. The goal is to practice critical thinking and analysis of data to explore how linear thinking may show up in the way a company operated and may have contributed to its failure. One example is Eastman Kodak, which was once a highly profitable producer of photographic film, eventually going through bankruptcy and massive shrinkage. What about the century-old hardware store that thrived until The Home Depot came to town? Also, it may question if failure for the company was hurtful for the community, environment, and Nature. In some cases, the effect may be quite positive. Some of the biggest coal mining firms have shrunk or ceased operations due to economics and expansion of renewable energy, a clear victory for the environment and human health.

Both exercises are helpful to lead to a **so-what step**, where students are invited to identify one way that they can and will change their own linear thinking with a direct impact on their behavior. This is an important part of both exercises because it helps connect their intellectual knowledge with relevant practical application. Making a public statement of the intention to change one's habit has a greater chance of being maintained. It is no longer a private decision, but something shared with a group, creating implicit accountability.

A story

Jack, a former VP of product development at a U.S. multinational corporation in the technology area shares a story that became a turning point for him and many of his colleagues. As part of a leadership development program, they were taken to a landfill, a place they had never set foot before. This was a typical open landfill of the 1990s. As the executives walked through piles of garbage and objects, they were speechless. They saw discarded office machines of their own brand, rusting as an unintentional and disorganized exhibition of our civilization's consumption. Products that they had carefully designed several years ago, made obsolete by successive newer designs, lay like lifeless testimonies of a business practice focused on the next product, the next sale, and the next competitive success. It was not just their own company's practices. The landfill laid bare the "business as usual" conduct of many well-known manufacturers of refrigerators, TV's, bottles, and plastics, jumbled together in large mountains.

The shocking experience had its effect. The leaders agreed that it was not possible to continue designing products that would become discarded material permanently adding to landfills for centuries. Something had to change. As a result, Jack and his team worked for seven years to invent and design a different approach to the technology business they were in.

Today this company has shifted its business model to renting and servicing equipment, retrieving the equipment at the end of lease contracts with their corporate clients. They brought new cyclical thinking to a traditional manufacturing model. This was not wholly the result of Jack's team, but their pioneering changes were the foundation of a mindset shift that brought further transformations, becoming a role model for the industry.

Other resources

Video about how energy flows and matter is recycled. https://www
.khanacademy.org/science/high-school-biology/hs-ecology/
trophic-levels/v/flow-of-energy-and-matter-through-
ecosystems

Video on 5 myths about Circular Economy. https://www.youtube
.com/watch?v=DGnfiBx7jK8

Free Guide for the Circular Economy. http://storage.googleapis
.com/www.bioregional.com/downloads/Cracking-the-circular-
challenge_Bioregional_2017_circular-economy.pdf

What causes Ocean Dead Zones? https://www.scientificamerican
.com/article/ocean-dead-zones/

Website The Story of Stuff, by Annie Leonard, has numerous short
videos. https://www.storyofstuff.org/

References

Ahn, S. H. & Lee, J. Y. (2018). Re-envisioning material circula-
tion and designing process in upcycling design product life cycle.
Archives of Design Research, *31*(4), 5–20.

Beckford, C. L., Jacobs, C., Williams, N., & Nahdee, R. (2010).
Aboriginal environmental wisdom, stewardship, and sustainability: Lessons from the Walpole Island first nations,
Ontario, Canada. *The Journal of Environmental Education*, *41*(4),
239–248.

Benyus, J. M. (1997). *Biomimicry: Innovation inspired by nature*. New
York, NY: Harper Collins.

Blühdorn, I. (2017). Post-capitalism, post-growth, post-consumer-
ism? Eco-political hopes beyond sustainability. *Global Discourse*,
7(1), 42–61.

Bocken, N. M., De Pauw, I., Bakker, C., & van der Grinten, B.
(2016). Product design and business model strategies for a circular
economy. *Journal of Industrial and Production Engineering*, *33*(5),
308–320.

Brown, C. (2017). *Buddhist economics: An enlightened approach to the
dismal science*. New York, NY: Bloomsbury Publishing.

Burns, H. L. (2015). Transformative sustainability pedagogy:
Learning from ecological systems and indigenous wisdom. *Journal
of Transformative Education*, *13*(3), 259–276.

Capra, F., & Luisi, P. L. (2014). *The systems view of life: A unifying vision.* Cambridge, UK: Cambridge University Press.

Demaria, F., Schneider, F., Sekulova, F., & Martinez-Alier, J. (2013). What is degrowth? From an activist slogan to a social movement. *Environmental Values, 22*(2), 191–215.

Drucker, P. F. (1994). *Post-capitalist society.* New York, NY: HarperCollins Publishers.

George, D. A., Lin, B. C. A., & Chen, Y. (2015). A circular economy model of economic growth. *Environmental Modelling & Software, 73,* 60–63.

Hendry, J. (2014). *Science and sustainability: Learning from indigenous wisdom.* New York, NY: Palgrave Macmillan.

Kallis, G. (2011). In defense of degrowth. *Ecological Economics, 70*(5), 873–880.

Kassel, K. (2013). *The thinking executive's guide to sustainability.* New York, NY: Business Expert Press.

Kirchherr, J., Reike, D., & Hekkert, M. (2017). Conceptualizing the circular economy: An analysis of 114 definitions. *Resources, Conservation and Recycling, 127,* 221–232.

Laszlo, E. (1989). *The inner limits of mankind: Heretical reflections on today's values, culture and politics.* Columbus, OH: Hallen Assoc.

Martinez-Alier, J. (2012). Environmental justice and economic degrowth: An alliance between two movements. *Capitalism Nature Socialism, 23*(1), 51–73.

McDonough, W. & Braungart, M. (2010). *Cradle to cradle: Remaking the way we make things.* San Francisco, CA: North Point Press.

McDonough, W. & Braungart, M. (2013). *The upcycle: Beyond sustainability–designing for abundance.* New York, NY: Macmillan.

Meadows, D. H., Meadows, D. L., Randers, J., & Behrens, W. W. (1972). *The limits to growth.* Washington, D.C.: Potomac Associates.

Moffitt, S. E., Hill, T. M., Roopnarine, P. D., & Kennett, J. P. (2015). Response of seafloor ecosystems to abrupt global climate change. *Proceedings of the National Academy of Sciences, 112*(15), 4684–4689.

Norberg-Hodge, H. (2009). *Ancient futures: Lessons from Ladakh for a globalizing world.* San Francisco, CA: Sierra Club Books.

O'Higgins, E. & Zsolnai, L. (Eds.) (2017). *Progressive business models: Creating sustainable and pro-social enterprise.* New York, NY: Springer.

Santha, S. D., Fraunholz, B., & Unnithan, C. (2010). A societal knowledge management system: Harnessing indigenous wisdom to build sustainable predictors for adaptation to climate change. *International Journal of Climate Change: Impacts and Responses*, 2(1), 49–64.

Schor, J. (2010). *Plenitude: The new economics of true wealth*. New York, NY: Penguin Press.

Setter, O. & Zsolnai, L. (Eds.) (2019). *Caring management in the new economy: Socially responsible behaviour through spirituality*. New York, NY: Springer.

Sung, K. & Sung, K. (2015). A review on upcycling: Current body of literature, knowledge gaps and a way forward. World Academy of Science, Engineering and Technology, Paris, France.

Weisman, A. (2008). *Gaviotas: A village to reinvent the world*. Hartford, VT: Chelsea Green Publishing.

Wilson, M. (2016). When creative consumers go green: Understanding consumer upcycling. *Journal of Product & Brand Management*, 25(4), 394–399.

Zsolnai, L. (2015). *Post-materialist business: Spiritual value-orientation in renewing management*. New York, NY: Springer.

7 Principle number 6

Interconnectedness

Definition

When we see interconnectedness, we understand the importance of diversity, and our decisions and actions become more inclusive, which contributes to the sustainability of the whole.

Teaching Goal

Students identify the complementary characteristics of differentiation and interconnectedness, developing inclusive decisions and actions that contribute to the sustainability of the whole.

Meta Goal

To develop the cognitive habit of thinking in terms of diversity and interconnectedness.

Origins of the Principle

Exploring the origins of "interconnectedness" takes us on a journey through history, with plenty of milestones and movements that alternate between periods of a holistic understanding of our interrelatedness and more siloed, fragmented views of the world. These cosmovisions influence how humans relate to each other and their environment, and their expressions can be seen in different disciplines: science, technology, philosophy, literature, arts, organization of society and states, etc. We will cite some of these cultural milestones.

For starters, while it may sound far-reaching, it is worth recalling studies showing that Neolithic civilizations in Old Europe, lasting for several thousand years, lived guided by a sense of interconnectedness with each other and the Earth. Archeologist Marija Gimbutas (1982), considered as a leading expert on Bronze Age Europe, found artifacts in major excavations on Southeastern Europe Neolithic sites from a nonhierarchical civilization that revered a female Earth Goddess as the creator of all interconnected existence. Gimbutas explored linguistics, archeology, housing patterns, social structures, art, and religion, and described a gynocentric peaceful society that honored equality, preceding the later androcentric, hierarchical societies. Her revolutionary work was highly appreciated by mythologist Joseph Campbell, although also questioned by her traditional archeology colleagues. Like her Neolithic predecessor, pre-Hellenic Greek Goddess Gaia also represented the Earth and all life, different from previous conceptions of human superiority. Indigenous cultures across the globe were held together by the understanding that humans, animals, and all Nature were connected. To this day, their statements and oral traditions seek to guide "white man" toward what seems a more resilient way of living with each other and Nature (LaDuke, 1994; Wall, 1993; Wall & Arden, 1990).

The holistic understanding of a spiritual connection with each other and with Nature is also a common foundation in religion and philosophy, including the influential Aristotelian philosophy, Christianity, the Jewish and Islamic religions, Vedic traditions, Taoism, Confucianism, and Buddhism. Authentic practice in the traditions and philosophies of world wisdom invites practitioners to reflect, ask critical questions, and derive creative solutions from the answers they receive in contemplation. When individuals practice meditation or silent contemplation, they connect with new insights about interconnected relationships emerging from their experience and knowledge, which is then translated into practical everyday wisdom.

And, yet about 500 years ago, a new worldview emerged in the Western hemisphere. Copernicus and Galileo challenged the Catholic hegemonic stance of an Earth-centric universe with their mathematical and astrological studies, facilitated by Kepler's invention of an improved telescope. Galileo advocated for measurable, quantitative methods, and advised against any qualitative observations based on the senses or nonrational methods (Capra, 1996, p 19). Descartes developed a rationalist view of the world, based on the analytical mind that could provide a better understanding—the only "right" understanding. The era of mind over matter had begun. Newton took it further, developing the mechanistic worldview, which described the world as a machine whose components could be studied independently. All of this is known as the Scientific Revolution, which marked the beginning of a reductionist, atomistic approach to science and knowledge. Bacon argued that rational thinking was in control as man now sought to establish "the power and dominion of the human race itself over the universe" (Merchant, 2008, p 736). Nature was seen as a female beast to be tamed (Merchant, 2008).

The Romantic Movement in Europe in the 18th and 19th centuries brought a reaction against this analytical way of understanding Nature through fragmentation. The rebellion stemmed from arts and literature with Goethe, Holderlin, Keats, Byron, Victor Hugo, and many others painting a world based on the senses and imagination, offering a more holistic understanding of the complexity of reality. In part, their voices were also reacting to the beginning of the Industrial Revolution.

Then by the mid–19th century, mechanistic thinking brought more inventions and progress through the development of the microscope, which led to an increased sense of human understanding (and feeling of control) over

Nature. Microbiology, Mendel's laws of heredity, and Darwin's theory of evolution were some of the discoveries that advanced the rationalistic method, and physics and chemistry became the building blocks for explaining entire organisms and their functions (Capra, 1996, p. 23).

The pendulum continued to swing and the next significant disruption came in the 1920s, with Heinberg's first descriptions of Quantum Physics. This revolutionary finding was that solid material objects actually dissolved at the subatomic level into wavelike patterns of probabilities (Capra, 1996, p. 30). The particles were no longer seen as isolated entities but existing only as interconnections among processes of observation and measurement. In Quantum Physics, the ending point is interconnecting waves, not material elementary units. One important significance of this new discovery was that it led to a shift from the reductionist, mechanistic approach to science through analysis, and fragmentation to a more holistic approach, where the whole is more than the sum of the parts.

Like a zeitgeist whose time had come, this holistic worldview spread across different disciplines. The General System Theory, postulated in the mid-1900s, described the world as composed of systems embedded in systems, interconnected in a network of mutually influencing relationships, and launched Systems Thinking (von Bertalanffy, 1968). In Psychology, the cognitive theory of Gestalt focused both on the *context* and the *properties* of the whole, leading to psychotherapeutic applications. In Biology, the school of Organicism (also called Vitalism) emerged, focusing on the study of interrelations and characteristics of the organism as a whole (Haraway, 1976). Organicism also became the foundation of Ecology, leading to the formulation of concepts such as the biosphere, and gave rise to James Lovelock's Gaia Hypothesis, which proposes that "all organisms and their inorganic surroundings on Earth are closely integrated to form a single and self-regulating complex system, maintaining the conditions for life on the planet."[1]

As an alternative to the quantitative scientific method, qualitative research surfaced, focusing on *why* things happen, rather than *how.* To this end, qualitative methods explore meanings, characteristics, symbols, and context, beyond numerical measurements. The renewed focus on context, leading to a more holistic understanding of the world, also began to appear in post-conventional think-ing as a characteristic within the stages of human devel-opment (Kohlberg, 1971). And more recently, efforts are being made to draw equal attention to objective and sub-jective research methods. Quantitative, qualitative, and mixed-method approaches are means for the examination of interconnected relationships between organisms and their ecological environments.

Why do we need this Principle?

Undoubtedly, the benefits of the rationalistic and reduc-tionist worldview in science were the significant discoveries and solutions developed, which improved our health and longevity through vaccines and early diagnoses and treat-ments, simplified our lives through technology, communi-cations, and transport, and led to many other innovations that impacted our lives for the better. At the same time, this worldview fostered an individualistic perspective, pro-moting values such as autonomy, independence, individual success, competition, personal achievement, and control. These values, broadly adopted in the Northern and Western hemispheres, also traveled and spread across more collec-tivistic cultures in the global South and East, particularly in the last decades of the 20th century.

When values become widely accepted, they shape a collective profile of identity, which may be more or less conscious. It becomes "the norm," like a widespread par-adigm that is no longer seen as an individual choice This particular paradigm—individualist, competitive, oriented toward growth, wealth, and accumulation—has also been linked to our unsustainability, as our behaviors become a (mostly unintentional) contribution to the problems we are experiencing (Rimanoczy, 2014). Charles Taylor (1991) argued that the contemporary focus on individualism has led to people experiencing a "disenchantment of the world" (p. 3). The experience of disenchantment leads to feeling disconnected from the world and, as a result, opportunities for authentic relationships suffer (Taylor, 1991). Several scholars observed this early on and referred to the urgent need to address a global mindset shift. Ervin Laszlo (1989), a member of the pioneering think tank Club of Rome, indicated that values are the "inner limits" of mankind at the core of our problems, meaning that our tacit values guide our behaviors and are creating the impacts we suffer—although we may not be aware of those linkages. Related theories evolved to include the evolutionary leap that man might make when he "awakens" his global brain to interconnectedness (Russell, 2000); the "Great Work" of transforming our consciousness (Berry, 2011); or how to move through the "Great Transition" (Raskin et al, 2002) by realizing how our thinking of separateness is shaping our problems.

Autonomy and independence may sound good, yet they are at odds with the laws of Nature, which is a web of interconnected organisms cooperating and mutually dependent beyond our imagination. Laszlo proposes to think of *interexistence*: "We may dream separately, but we must act together" (p. 109). Csikszentmihalyi (1993, p. 156–157) suggests that evolutionary complexity is the result of an increase in differentiation and integration, which are complementary aspects: "*Differentiation refers to the degree to which a system (an organ, an individual, a family, a corporation, a culture or humanity as a whole) is composed of parts that differ in structure or function from one another. Integration refers to the extent to which the different parts communicate and enhance one another's goals.*"

This is similar to the cells in our body, which have differentiated structures and functions yet operate in an integrated way to perform their role. None of them taken independently would be able to survive outside of the whole. This became obvious to all of us as the Coronavirus started to spread. Suddenly we realized that beyond our differences we shared a physical constitution that made us prone to get the virus. And if we didn't take care of each other by staying at home and practicing the hygienic recommendations, we would not be able to survive. Nature is organized in nested, interconnected systems, yet our human creations seem to be built outside of this rule as if this were possible. They may survive in the short term, but as we now realize, this is merely a myopic, anthropocentric aspiration. Whether we plan on it or ignore it, we still are interconnected.

This is closely related to the stakeholder theory developed by Freeman, who realized how many social and environmental problems might be addressed if we had a more inclusive approach to stakeholders' perspectives, going beyond the profit-oriented interests of shareholders (Freeman, Wicks, & Parmar, 2004; Hörisch, Freeman, & Schaltegger, 2014). The need to shift the individualistic paradigm also was addressed in the theory of Buddhist Economics, which has the Principle of interconnectedness at its foundation (Brown, 2017).

In view of its wide implications, from science to technology developments to business innovations and policy decisions, the Principle of Interconnectedness seems to be at the intersection of multiple disciplines that can positively impact the sustainability of our planet. As with the previous Principles, this one has in common the leverage potential of impacting our thinking, our values, and our decisions. By developing habits of mind that spontaneously include the understanding of holistic interconnections, we may be acting more efficiently to shape the world we want to live in.

How is this Principle effectively brought into the classroom?

This Principle is translated into the following Goals:

Teaching Goal:

Students identify the complementary aspects of differentiation and interconnectedness, developing inclusive decisions and actions that contribute to the sustainability of the whole.

Meta Goal:

To develop the cognitive habit of thinking in terms of diversity and interconnectedness.

It is easy to feel overwhelmed by the philosophical origins of the Principles, and this one is no exception. The wide-ranging explorations of this Principle, across time and disciplines, may make us lose sight of what we can do in the limited setting of a classroom or a workshop. The purpose of the teaching goal is to reset the focus and provide simple questions and suggestions to create learning activities that can have a powerful impact on the mindset.

In this case, the teaching goal involves introducing opportunities to notice how all is connected, how diversity represents richness and yet has to be complemented by integration (inclusion) to properly function. Making the links to daily decisions will help students learn to "see" when interconnectedness solves problems, and when ignoring it creates them. Once again, the COVID-19 crisis can be a handy teaching resource, since every individual independently of career or location will have some vivid, personal stories to relate. COVID-19 brought with it many things, and the lesson of interdependency was one.

The meta goal will be met if, by repetition and practice, students develop a new habit, and it becomes their automatic way of looking at information and making decisions.

Key components

The key components in this Principle are as follows:

- *Interconnections as a law of Systems thinking*
- *Interconnectedness as a Spiritual teaching*
- *Interconnectedness as a Biological principle*
- *Interconnectedness in our values: Interdependence versus autonomy and independence*
- *Sustainable Development Goals (SDGs)*
- *Stakeholders*

As shown in the previous sections, there are many avenues to introduce this Principle of Interconnectedness. The rationale for listing several of them as key components is to broaden the student's perspective, illustrating the wide-reaching origins of this Principle.

For *Systems thinking*, the Principle can be introduced through the systems theoretical framework, and in the Resources section, you will find several links to platforms and sites with articles, slides, and videos, in addition to exercises. Interconnectedness as a *Spiritual teaching* can be introduced by having students reflect on their own spiritual upbringing, or on different religious traditions, and to seek out how and why this Principle is included therein. This may bring up angles such as "man taming Nature" or "man as 'steward' of Nature," which opens up for an interesting exploration of the values behind the terms.

The *Biological perspective* is particularly valuable for students in disciplines that have little or no connection with Biology. How is interconnectedness found in living life forms, and what metaphors does it offer for their discipline?

At a more personal level, the exploration of the culturally accepted values of *autonomy and independence* are a rich path to explore the ways in which we are unintentionally ignoring the connections. This can be introduced after exploring the concept of interconnectedness, which probably will have led students to see the importance of the Principle. To realize that they are actually *not* acting with that in mind, is a powerful *AHA!* moment that can trigger a transformative learning experience. One exercise can be to **Scrutinize Independence**, by inviting the students to list the situations in which they are independent and happy to be so, and then analyze it from the perspective of this Principle.

Another activity at the *personal* level can be to invite students to reflect what situation in their current life is causing them trouble because they are not considering this Principle.

The *SDGs* are another key component, given the fact that they apply to any discipline. Every one of us has some role to play to help achieve them and to explore how the SDGs are by themselves interconnected provides students with a broader perspective of the complex challenges we have to solve—and also of the many leverage points we have because of said interconnectedness.

Finally, independently of the discipline that is being taught, the concept of *stakeholders* is a very useful way to develop awareness of the richness of diversity and the need to create ways to keep in mind and include the different voices. Stakeholders illustrate the importance and power of differentiation and integration.

Preparing yourself for the task

Key questions for the educator:

For self-awareness:

- How am I personally experiencing this Principle in my own life? At the biological, intuitive, spiritual level, perhaps?

- When is my drive for autonomy and independence at odds with this Principle? How do I solve it and/or deal with it?

To prepare the assignments/activities:

- What are the positive aspects and what are the downsides of the idea that everything (and everyone) is interconnected?
- Where does the concept (value) of autonomy and independence come from?
- Connect with identity: How is autonomy and independence an anchor of our identity? Be prepared to explore feelings related to this Principle.

Tips for the educator:

- The conversation can remain at an intellectual level until we address **values that anchor our identity**. When we talk about autonomy, independence, control, or personal achievement, there will be different feelings associated with these. It is useful to remember that the more our identity is anchored in external aspects (conditions of belonging and being accepted, expected roles, etc.) the more this identity becomes a precious possession to defend. Seek, therefore, to make this a dialog, without the need to advocate, to convince others, or to make a decision about what is "right" and what is "wrong." We are in the internal dimension, the seat of values and beliefs, and these only evolve and change slowly, at a personal pace, and when the timing is right for the individual. The best goal to achieve will be to expand awareness, not to change the values that students hold dearly.
- What reflections can the students extract from their **COVID-19 experience**, related to interconnectedness? How did they feel the interdependency, how did

they react, and act? What remained of this lesson with the passage of time? Was it transformative?

An exercise to try out

The shirt exercise[2]

Ask the students where the shirt they are wearing comes from, if they did not make the shirt themselves. From their response you begin to take it outward: Who played a role in them wearing this shirt? They can work in duos or trios to list in a limited time (5 minutes) all the possible people who intervened.

Then the students read out loud their list, without repeating what others already mentioned. The scope can go very far:

*   Those intervening with the materials used to make the shirt;
*   the building in which it was made;
*   the truck to ship the shirts;
*   the packaging to ship the shirts;
*   the boats to ship the shirts;
*   the places that build the boats;
*   the harbor on both (the departing and the arriving) coasts;
*   trucks on both coasts;
*   the mall;
*   the store that sells the shirts;
*   the materials to build the malls; and
*   employees to work in the stores, etc.

After listening to each other, they get the sense of how unlimited and far-reaching the list goes, getting the experience of how we are all interdependent and interconnected. You can take the dialog toward the question of how do values such as autonomy and independence play in this context.

A story

I was teaching at Al-Akhwayn University, Morocco. I wanted to introduce the Principle of Interconnectedness, but the students seemed distracted, absent-minded, overly connected to their phones. It was clear to me that they were enduring the last hour of class in midst of the Ramadan season, which means that they were tired, thirsty, hungry, and ready to go home and sleep until the fasting time was over. I decided to ask them to open on their phones or laptops the websites of the BBC, Aljazeera, and the London Times, dividing the group, respectively. The assignment was to find in a very limited time (5 minutes) as many news clips in that media that showed the lack of consideration to the Principle of Interconnectedness.

Then they had to share how many they found and also explain in what ways the Principle was not taken into account.

The atmosphere quickly livened up, driven by competition and time pressure. I thought that the time frame was too short to derive any significant reflections, but I was surprised to see how they spontaneously could explain how the news might be a problem because of the lack of stakeholder engagement, independent of the circumstances. What this exercise showed me is that they didn't have to pause and study the news to find this Principle (and its impact), but rather that they had already embedded a new habit of mind, proven by the fact that they could easily contribute the explanation.

Other resources

Graph and Article about Systems thinking. https://medium.com/disruptive-design/tools-for-systems-thinkers-the-6-fundamental-concepts-of-systems-thinking-379cdac3dc6a

Resources about Systems Thinking. https://thesystemsthinker.com/

Notes

1. https://courses.seas.harvard.edu/climate/eli/Courses/
   EPS281r/Sources/Gaia/Gaia-hypothesis-wikipedia.pdf
   Retrieved Feb 16 2020.
2. This exercise is adapted from an exercise used by Michael
   Lees with his students to develop a sense of interdependence,
   social, cultural, economic, ecological impact, and karma.
   He calls it a "micro < > macro" approach to understanding
   impact and what sustainability looks like relative in the macro
   context of the act of purchasing a t-shirt.

References

Berry, T. (2011). *The great work: Our way into the future*. New York,
NY: Crown Publishing Group.

Brown, C. (2017). *Buddhist economics: An enlightened approach to the
dismal science*. New York, NY: Bloomsbury Publishing USA.

Capra, F. (1996). *The web of life*. New York, NY: Anchor Book.

Csikszentmihalyi, M. (1993). *The evolving self: A psychology for the
third millennium*. New York, NY: HarperCollins.

Freeman, R. E., Wicks, A. C., & Parmar, B. (2004). Stakeholder theory and "the corporate objective revisited". *Organization Science,
15*(3), 364–369.

Gimbutas, M. (1982). *The goddesses and gods of Old Europe, 6500-3500
BC, myths and cult images*. Berkeley, CA: University of California
Press.

Haraway, D. J. (1976). *Crystals, Fabrics, and Fields: Metaphors of organicism in twentieth-century developmental biology*. New Haven, CT:
Yale University Press.

Hörisch, J., Freeman, R. E., & Schaltegger, S. (2014). Applying
stakeholder theory in sustainability management: Links, similar-
ities, dissimilarities, and a conceptual framework. *Organization &
Environment, 27*(4), 328–346.

Kohlberg, L. (1971). Stages of moral development. *Moral Education,
1*(51), 23–92.

LaDuke, W. (1994). Traditional ecological knowledge and environmental futures. *Colorado Journal of International Environmental Law
and Policy, 5*, 127.

Laszlo, E. (1989). *The inner limits of mankind: Heretical reflections on
today's values, culture and politics*. London: Oneworld Publications.

Merchant, C. (2008). "The Violence of Impediments": Francis Bacon and the origins of experimentation. *Isis 99*(4), 731–760.

Raskin, P., Banuri, T., Gallopin, G., Gutman, P., Hammond, A., Kates, R., & Swart, R. (2002). *Great transition: The promise and lure of the times ahead*. Boston, MA: Stockholm Environmental Institute.

Rimanoczy, I. (2014). A matter of being: Developing sustainability-minded leaders. *Journal of Management for Global Sustainability*, 2(1), 95–122.

Russell, P. (2000). *The global brain awakens: Our next evolutionary leap*. Boston, MA: Element Books.

Taylor, C. (1991). *The ethics of authenticity*. Cambridge, MA: Harvard University Press.

Von Bertalanffy, L. (1968). General system theory—a critical review. *Modern systems research for the behavioral scientist* (pp. 11–30). Chicago, IL: *Aldine*.

Wall, S. (1993). *Wisdom's daughters: Conversations with women elders of native America*. New York, NY: Harper Collins.

Wall, S. & Arden, H. (1990). *Wisdomkeepers: Meetings with native American spiritual elders*. New York, NY: Atria Books.

Part IV

Emotional Intelligence

We are now entering the third content area: Emotional Intelligence. Emotional Intelligence has been defined through abilities (Salovey & Mayer, 1990), traits (Petrides & Furnham, 2000), or a combination of both (Goleman, 1995). In the framework of the Sustainability Mindset, we refer to Emotional Intelligence as "the ability to monitor one's own and others' feelings and emotions, to discriminate among them, and to use this information to guide one's thinking and actions" (Salovey and Mayer, 1990, p.189). The concept of Emotional Intelligence covers a broad spectrum related to understanding and regulating feelings and behaviors; however, the particular connection with the Sustainability Mindset is that Emotional Intelligence facilitates individual adaptation and change and increases the likelihood for organizations (or rather their members) to realize radical change (Huy, 1999, p.325). There is no debate about the urgent need of *radical changes*.

In my research of sustainability-minded pioneers, I found three aspects within the content area of Emotional Intelligence that played a pivotal role in the mindset shift of each individual: The openness to *creative innovation*, the practice of *reflection*, and the interest in deepening *self-awareness*. These are the three Principles introduced in this section.

While these are not the only aspects of Emotional Intelligence that may contribute to a mindset for sustainability, they were significant in the study used to develop the concept of the Sustainability Mindset. They have since been used in developing the mindset with many students in different contexts and have been shown to contribute to accelerating their mindset shift. The exercises and activities focusing on creative innovation, reflection, and self-awareness are powerful in their impact and yet relatively simple to implement, thus they are stated as Principles.

References

Goleman, D. (1995). *Emotional intelligence*. New York, NY: Bantam Books.

Huy, Q. (1999). Emotional capability, emotional intelligence, and radical change. *Academy of Management Review, 24*(2), 325–345.

Petrides, K., & Furnham, A. (2000). On the dimensional structure of emotional intelligence. *Personality and Individual Differences, 29*(2), 313–320.

Salovey, P. & Mayer, J. D. (1990). Emotional intelligence. *Imagination, Cognition and Personality, 9*(3), 185–211.

8 Principle number 7
Creative innovation

Definition

Resilience is based on constant creativity, innovation, and experimentation. When we neglect the nonrational wisdom we have in us, our solutions are missing critical information and may create negative impacts on the ecosystem and society.

Teaching Goal

Students learn to connect resiliency with innovation, identify the value of nonverbal intuitive wisdom, and enhance their personal potential for creative imagination.

Meta Goal

To develop self-confidence both in listening to their intuitive voice and in their (urgently needed) capacity to be creative.

Origins of the Principle

In this section, we will explore how creative processes and experimentation can result in innovation and resilience. We define human creativity as the ability to connect with our intuitive knowledge and aesthetics, activating our imagination. Innovation is creativity in action, the ability to experiment with new ways of doing things and solving problems. Resilience, according to Wesley-Esquimaux (2009), is the ability to rebound from challenges in everyday life and to recover from and survive adversarial conditions.

Let's start with Nature. In his book *The Web of Life* (1996), Fritjof Capra notes that creativity is a key property of all living systems. Creativity is expressed in the generation of biodiversity that has been taking place over billions of years in an uninterrupted process of unfolding life (p. 221). The ecosystem has evolved and developed, thanks to a combination of competition and cooperation, creation, and adaptation. Genetics researchers state that creative innovation also emerges as a resilient response to catastrophes: planetary breaking points are followed by intense periods of growth and innovation. For example, the depletion of hydrogen in the Earth's atmosphere over two billion years ago led to a major innovation: The use of water in photosynthesis. Millions of years later, the accumulation of toxic oxygen prompted the evolution of oxygen-breathing bacteria (Capra, 1996, p. 232; Margulis & Sagan 1986).

The resilience of the world's indigenous tribes is an excellent example of how a combination of adaptation and creativity resulted in their thousands of years of existence. As Canadian scholar and native Anishinaabe community member McGuire-Kishebakabaykwe (2010, p. 118) wrote: "We left the place where we lived in the same condition that we found it." Resilience is not just an observed characteristic of today's indigenous populations, but a core aspect of their existence and much can be learned from them for our management for sustainability (Rotarangi & Russell, 2009).

Resilience can also be observed in circumstances of disaster. Similar to that described in the resilience of Nature, devastating events have been seen to awaken social sensitivity, empathy, and willingness to help others (Aldrich, 2012; Nemeth & Olivier, 2017). On a less scholarly and more empirical level, the dramatic spread of the Coronavirus began awakening the compassion and social sensitivity of communities around the globe. China shipped ventilators and medical material to Italy in the midst of their health crisis, while Russia and Cuba sent hundreds of epidemiologists to support the Italian doctors. People in Buenos Aires and Spain clapped in appreciation to the health workers every day at 8 pm from their balconies, and the Internet exploded in advice and encouragement to friends and strangers.

Arnold Toynbee, studying the rise and fall of civilizations, indicates that the critical element in the collapse of a culture is the loss of flexibility. When behaviors and social norms become rigid, individuals are so focused on holding on to what they know that they lose the ability to adapt to changing contexts. This creates the breakdown and disintegration of a society or civilization. Versatility and flexibility are essential traits of resilient societies and result when structures and institutions make room for experimentation and creative innovation (Capra, 1983, p. 28). But it should be noted that it is not organizations that are flexible; rather it is individuals that take the lead and influence structures and processes. Toynbee notes that creative minorities will appear in the midst of rigid societies and challenge the status quo. They may be rejected by the system, but within a larger time span their impact will be noted. If the time span is too long, the institutions may disintegrate, and the pioneering minorities may create new configurations (Capra, 1983, p. 29).

In terms of individual development, Piaget depicts the combination of assimilation and accommodation as the interaction of the individual with the environment, an essential aspect of cognitive intelligence (Block, 1982; Huitt & Hummel, 2003). In sustainability management, we are familiar with the terms "preventive action" and "adaptive changes," which similarly refer to (preventive) actions to influence or transform the environment, or to how we adapt our lives to what we cannot change. Both, however, call for creative innovation, since we have to develop new habits, behaviors, technologies, and processes.

At this point, it is necessary to introduce Emotional Intelligence as a complement to the cognitive view of intelligence. The traditional view of intelligence relates to the ability to learn, understand, use logical thinking, solve problems, and use language to communicate. These abilities have been measured through intelligence tests, although in recent decades the concept of intelligence has been expanded to include multiple intelligences: Emotional, spatial, kinesthetic, musical, interpersonal, and intrapersonal (Gardner, 2011; Goleman, 1995). Gardner's different types of intelligence have been criticized because they have not been measured (Morgan, 1996; Peariso, 2008); however, they certainly address human adaptive and creative skills beyond the verbal and numerical functions. In fact, studies have shown that a higher Emotional Intelligence correlates with more conscious decisions, encompassing both emotional and rational components (Mayer, 2008)—which is noteworthy as it means that individuals developing their Emotional Intelligence may be able to create more sustainable innovations. Furthermore, a study with 488 Italian workers, aged 18 to 55, demonstrated that Emotional Intelligence is an antecedent to, or prerequisite for, resilience (Magnano, Craparo, & Paolillo, 2016).

Why do we need this Principle?

Our planetary challenges require that we globally rethink and reinvent how we produce, consume, and distribute products; how we eat, dress, and entertain ourselves; and how we shelter 9.2 billion people on the planet by 2040. It is not enough to have a temporary halt in our environmental footprint due to country lockdowns—we need to develop new ways of going about our daily lives without the negative footprint we are making. Creativity, resourcefulness, and innovation will be essential to face this monumental endeavor (Ehrenfeld, 2009). There is not a single profession exempt from the need to reinvent itself.

Architecture, product manufacturing, farming, governance, services, health, communications, transportation, education—the list has no end.

In the previous section, we have seen the correlation of utilizing emotional intelligence and resilience, and non-verbal, nonrational knowing to develop creative, innovative solutions for the planetary challenges we face. Albert Einstein noted that the intellect has little to do with the road to discovery. So the question is how do we access that *other* way of knowing? How do we foster and develop it?

There is a widespread myth that creativity is not a generalized attribute of humankind, but a rare gift that certain individuals possess (Kelley & Kelley, 2013). Yet, as children, we all are spontaneously creative and inventive, and we don't think of this as a special gift. We simply experiment and play. Schooling then begins to prioritize logical and rational functions, rewarding our analytical, mathematical, or verbal performance, while imagination and "nonsense" are pushed aside (with the exception of some particular educational institutions, like those based on the pedagogies of Maria Montessori and Rudolf Steiner). Following the human need to perform for and meet the expectations of others and given the existing social reward system promoting rational thinking, we become adults who, generally speaking, don't see themselves as gifted for creativity. This is definitely a self-limiting belief and a major obstacle in the way of the innovation required for the challenges we have to collectively address.

Many educational institutions are actively focusing on preparing students to be responsible leaders and to develop sustainable behaviors in the next generation. Social entrepreneurship is encouraged, and small and medium enterprises are seen as key potential champions of change. However, entrepreneurship is more than resources and capabilities. It requires innovation to thrive in a globally competitive environment where uncertainty and ambiguity are the norms. Entrepreneurship calls for creativity to adapt to changes and develop new value (Ngah, Abd Wahab, & Salleh, 2015).

In my research, leaders repeatedly shared their concern that as they were seeking solutions to sustainability problems, they couldn't find benchmarks or examples of how others had solved them. They realized that if something had to change, they would need to be the ones to invent it—which meant stepping aside from the existing "efficient" processes, promoting a culture of experimentation and trial-and-learning, and accepting the possibility of failures on the road to innovation.

Being open to the uncertainty of experimentation and creativity, to the divergent thinking that seems inefficient, and to intuitive knowing is important, since they are key aspects of the Sustainability Mindset. If we want to build a resilient life on this planet, we need to tap into other ways of knowing to complement our "efficient" and rational processes. There is a substantial need for innovation and creativity in the design of human–Nature relationships in order to invent sustainable lifestyles and enterprises (Ehrenfeld, 2009). We need to create conditions to unleash students' imagination and develop self-confidence in their knowledge that they have all they need to be creative and invent new ways of doing things.

Shrivastava suggests the use of art as a pedagogical resource, as it provides a direct line to human emotions and can be valuable in our pursuit of sustainability (Shrivastava, 2010). Furthermore, art engages emotions, passion, and compassion, and can trigger solutions that bring about real changes (Shrivastava, Ivanaj, & Ivanaj, 2012).

Csikszentmihalyi (1993, p. 176) describes the sense of "flow" present in the creative acts, with emotions such as absorption, involvement, joy, or sense of accomplishment. We have all experienced this at some time: Whether it was playing with a child, cooking, gardening, listening to or playing music, dancing, playing with a pet, or running a marathon. How can we help students identify moments when they were in the flow and connected to their intuitive wisdom?

This Principle provides a guide to help educators in any discipline to find new ways of developing creativity and innovation with their students. This will mean incorporating activities or situations where students can both understand the need for innovation and uncover their dormant creativity.

How is this Principle effectively brought into the classroom?

This Principle is translated into the following Goals:

Teaching Goal:

> *Students learn to connect resiliency with innovation, identify the value of nonverbal intuitive wisdom, and enhance their personal potential for creative imagination.*

Meta Goal:

> *To develop self-confidence in listening to their intuitive voice and in their (urgently needed) capacity to be creative.*

It may be challenging to personally realize that the need for innovation exists in every discipline, including our area of expertise, and that we all have dormant creativity, veiled in many cases with a layer of mistrust in our own capacity to imagine. This teaching goal calls first for the educator to come to terms with his or her own mindset related to creativity and "other ways of knowing." This Principle can be introduced with information, but ultimately has to address the nonrational ways of knowing. As we move through the content areas of Emotional and Spiritual Intelligence, it not only becomes more personal for the students, but also for the educator, who may face the challenge and benefits of stepping out of the comfort zone.

The teaching goal involves connecting resiliency with innovation, for which fortunately we now have a large number of inspiring cases and benchmarks across disciplines. Other ways of knowing and personal beliefs of what creativity means are best accessed through experiential learning, art, journaling, and dialogs. These are also useful tools to achieve the meta goal of developing self-confidence. A project where the students can get involved in making a difference is a great pedagogical resource that combines experiential learning, innovation, reflection, and self-awareness, as we can see in the Story featured at the end of this chapter.

Key components

The key components in this Principle are as follows:

- *Resilience in Nature*
- *Resilience in ancestral, aboriginal, and native wisdom*
- *Lessons from Nature and native wisdom about resilience in our discipline*
- *Art as an aesthetic experience of intuitive knowing*
- *Who is creative? Uncovering the self-limiting thoughts*
- *What needs to be reinvented?*

Resilience is a noninvasive place to start, because it can be explored in analytical and intellectual ways. Independent of the discipline being taught, starting with a brief exploration of how resilience is present *in Nature* and the four-billion-year trajectory of our Earth can be a powerful platform for discussion. What aspects of adaptation, collaboration, competition, and recreation can we link with our current civilization? What aspects are we neglecting that may be at the root of our unsustainability as humanity?

Introducing the students *to ancestral or aboriginal wisdom* is the next strategy that can illustrate what it looks like when humans are in harmony with Nature (Fleming & Ledogar,

2008). This may be a distant scenario from urban living contexts, but it is worthwhile to explore, given the thousands of years of successful adaptation and survival (Rival, 2009). Even the demise of the Rapa-Nui civilization on Easter Island, long attributed to their overconsumption of natural resources, has recently been disproved as evidence was found that the Rapa Nui had, in fact, been victims of diseases brought in by the Europeans (Mulrooney, 2012; Peiser, 2005).

A bridge can be built between the resilience of Nature and that of aboriginal peoples and the implications *to the discipline that is being taught* to students. Where is the unsustainability linked to a lack of proper adaptation to changing environments? Where are organizations or systems clinging to their "ways of doing," despite undesirable impacts? What is the role of individuals in promoting innovation and new ways of looking at things? What are the obstacles to be expected, as we propose new ways of seeing and thinking?

There is a recent movement promoting *art as a pedagogical tool* to connect management students with sustainability, particularly via the nonverbal, holistic aesthetic experience (Ivanaj, Poldner, & Shrivastava, 2014; Lineberry & Wiek, 2016; Yang, Ivanova, & Hufnagel, 2019). This includes experiential learning (i.e., visits to museums, art galleries, artist meetings), crafting art (digital portfolios, photography, poetry, painting, collage), or other performance expressions (improvisation, dance, music). It is essential to complement art-related experience with journaling or reflective essays in order to allow students to extract meaning and deepen their intuitive experience. Also research on intuition has expanded, exploring its role in the creative process and decision making, among other areas (Sinclair, 2010, 2014). Some leading institutional pioneers in this approach are the MiL Institute in Sweden, Schumacher College in UK, and the IEDC-Bled School of Management, Slovenia.

Dialogs about what creativity means for students—who is creative and who might not be—are rich ways to *uncover self-limiting thoughts* and explore their origins in the personal history of the student. Assignments and reflective essays to explore "when did I stop being creative," as well as peer learning, can help individuals reconnect with their dormant creativity. Expanding the concept of creativity beyond the arts is important since we are creative when we organize a birthday party, when we make a salad, when we combine colors in our wardrobe, when we decorate our home, and when we work in our garden.

Finally, a conversation to explore what has to be reinvented in the world, in the classroom, or in the profession related to the discipline we are teaching are valuable ways to ground the Principle into concrete actions. *What can I do?*

Preparing yourself for the task

Key questions for the educator:

For self-awareness:

- How am I listening to my intuition? What are my obstacles against it?
- What happens when I listen to my gut feeling?
- How do I see myself in terms of creativity? What are my limiting thoughts?
- Did I lose my creativity? If so, when?
- How do I best express myself creatively?

To prepare the assignments/activities:

- What are the downsides of innovation?
- What are some criteria for innovation in service of the greater good/of the planet?
- How does innovation relate to impact on stakeholders (Principle Interconnections), to long-term thinking and to both+and thinking?

- How does this Principle connect with the discipline you are teaching? Establish those connections first before seeking activities.

Tips for the educator:

- **Breaking a habit:** Keep in mind that most students have been rewarded for their linear, analytical thinking, and less so for their out-of-the-box, creative expressions. Be patient.
- **Respect the self-image:** Do students recognize their own creativity? It is worth exploring their assumptions and limiting beliefs related to creative people. Their self-image may be linked to being pragmatic, no-nonsense, and rational (even at the cost of admitting "zero creativity"). This is something to challenge, but it will also impact how they see themselves. Find fun and indirect ways to address this, for example, using music, movies, cooking, story-telling, creating a You-Tube video, or visiting an art exhibition.
- **Expand the concept:** Creativity can be found in daily situations, such as organizing a vacation or a party, or in performance-related hobbies, and not only in artistic expressions. Use space to provide a setting conducive to creativity, for example, meeting in a park or a coffee shop instead of the classroom, or simply sitting in a circle.
- **Dealing with resistance:** Connecting creative expression with entrepreneurial innovation can help lower resistance. Aim2Flourish.com is a rich platform with hundreds of current examples from around the world.
- **In the news:** Are there any recent innovations in the news that can be discussed/analyzed from the perspective of impact?

An exercise to try out

E-Portfolio: *Using contemplative photography to foster a sustainability mindset*[1]

The digital-native generation of students is so addicted to mobile phones that it is often difficult for the students to switch them off during class. Using phones for taking pictures and posting them on Instagram or sharing them with friends and family through social messaging is a daily routine for most modern students. Given this popularity of digital photography among students, innovative educator Chulguen Yang, professor in the Management Department at Southern Connecticut State University, proposed that this simplest of art forms could be used to cultivate aesthetic sensitivity, boost creative potential, and develop the contemplative skills of business students. A number of scholars in Russia, Germany, and South Africa have followed this initiative: They've adopted the E-Portfolio project assignment as an impactful pedagogical tool in the management classroom in order to cultivate the sustainability mindset of their students. At the beginning of the course, students are informed about the E-Portfolio as an individual project assignment and provided with the instructions regarding how they can use their existing archives of digital photos or create a set of 30 contemplative photos, to reflect on the interconnectedness of the themes of sustainability, art, and nature. Students are asked to prepare an E-Portfolio that consists of three components: (1) a 1,000-word prolog that describes their approach to the assignment and understanding of the three themes; (2) 30 digital photographs with some background information (e.g., name, date, location); and (3) a 1,500-word epilog with reflection upon the operationalization of their E-Portfolios, the process of selecting or taking the contemplative photographs, and the derived meaning at the personal level on the proposed three themes. Students are given a sufficient amount of time to complete the assignment and at the end of the course, after submitting their E-Portfolios, each student delivers a five-minute presentation on the content of their E-Portfolio and the insights that this assignment provoked. Most of students appreciate an opportunity to reflect on their life experience through their own photographs and admit that it was one of the most engaging learning activities offered to them in their studies.

A story

Some years ago I was teaching a course on the Sustainability Mindset at the International School of Hospitality and Tourism Management at Fairleigh Dickinson University in New Jersey. The design included several different activities to unleash the students' imagination, awaken their dormant creativity, and realize the importance of reinventing "everything." Some of the activities included collage, mind-maps, poetry, music, and a picnic with traditional ethnic foods since the students came from many different countries. Students also had to identify a project to start and finish during the semester, something that would make a positive difference in the school, community, or the world.

One of the students, Jacqueline, was increasingly concerned about the lack of a "sustainability awareness" in the school. The more she learned about the state of the planet and developed a shift in her mindset, the more she worried about this missing piece in the school's programs. She couldn't see why a program that taught how to manage tourism and hotels would not be connected with the responsibility of the professionals they were forming to shape a better world. Or to lower the ecological footprint, at the very least. She asked: What if we had a professional Oath that students could take voluntarily at graduation, committing to a sustainability-responsible professional performance? Jacqueline ran the idea by several professors, by peers, and then by the Dean. After she received encouragement to do so, she crafted a draft of the Oath and shared it again to obtain input. Finally, with the approval of several professors and authorities, she had the final version. She was the first one launching this Oath, taking it herself at graduation.

The Oath started with this statement:

> I, (name), as an International School of Hospitality and Tourism Management graduate at Fairleigh Dickinson University, acknowledge my role in society.

> My purpose is:

- To faithfully and conscientiously fulfill my duties as an industry professional to the best of my abilities and uphold its beliefs and practices;
- To make decisions based on the well-being of individuals in my endeavors today and in the future; and
- To make an active effort to create and achieve a sustainable and inclusive economic, social, and environmental global society.

This was followed by 10 promises (e.g., I will start and continue my journey to maintain the balance of natural resources by considering the impact of my actions on the environment, society, and economy; I will promote and support my local farmers, markets, and networks to benefit my local thriving community).

She saw this innovation as a way to draw the attention of other graduates to their opportunities to shape a better world, thus developing their consciousness. Intentions stated publicly have greater chances to influence and guide behaviors and decisions.

Other resources

The work of Chuck Hoberman (see http://www.hoberman.com) is a good example of the subtle fusion of art, science, and architecture to serve sustainability.

TED Talk: A call to artists for sustainable development, by Alice Audouin. https://www.ted.com/talks/alice_audouin_appel_aux_artistes_pour_le_developpement_durable?utm_campaign=ted spread&utm_medium=referral&utm_source=tedcomshare

TED Talk: Using Nature's genius as inspiration for architecture by Michael Pawlyn. https://www.ted.com/talks/michael_pawlyn_using_nature_s_genius_in_architecture?utm_campaign=ted spread&utm_medium=referral&utm_source=tedcomshare

TED Talk: Would you live in a floating city in the sky? By Tomas Saraceno. https://www.ted.com/talks/tomas_saraceno_would_you_live_in_a_floating_city_in_the_sky?utm_campaign=ted spread&utm_medium=referral&utm_source=tedcomshare

TED Talk: The beautiful future of solar power by Marjan van Aubel. https://www.ted.com/talks/marjan_van_aubel_the_beautiful_future_of_solar_power?utm_campaign=tedspread&utm_medi um=referral&utm_source=tedcomshare

Note

1. Thanks to Dr. Ekaterina Ivanova who contributed this exercise she uses with her students at the Department of Strategic and International Management of the National Research University "Higher School of Economics" in Moscow, Russia.

References

Aldrich, D. P. (2012). Social capital in post disaster recovery: Towards a resilient and compassionate East Asian Community. In Y. Sawada & S. Oum (Eds.), *Economic and welfare impacts of disasters in East Asia and policy responses* (pp. 157–178). ERIA Research Project Report 2011-8, Jakarta, Indonesia: ERIA.

Block, J. (1982). Assimilation, accommodation, and the dynamics of personality development. *Child Development*, 53, 281–295.

Capra, F. (1983). *The turning point: Science, society, and the rising culture.* New York, NY: Bantam Books.

Capra, F. (1996). *The web of life.* New York, NY: Anchor Book.

Csikszentmihalyi, M. (1993). *The evolving self: A psychology for the third millennium.* New York NY: HarperCollins.

Ehrenfeld, J. (2009). *Sustainability by design.* New Haven, CT: Yale University Press.

Fleming, J. & Ledogar, R. J. (2008). Resilience, an evolving concept: A review of literature relevant to aboriginal research. *Pimatisiwin: A Journal of Aboriginal and Indigenous Community Health, 6*(2), 7–24.

Gardner, H. (2011). *Frames of mind: The theory of multiple intelligences.* London: Hachette.

Goleman, D. (1995). *Emotional intelligence.* New York, NY: Bantam Books.

Huitt, W. & Hummel, J. (2003). Piaget's theory of cognitive development. *Educational Psychology Interactive, 3*(2), 1–5.

Ivanaj, V., Poldner, K., & Shrivastava, P. (2014). Hand/heart/head: Aesthetic practice pedagogy for deep sustainability learning. *Journal of Corporate Citizenship,* 54, 23–46.

Kelley, T. & Kelley, D. (2013). *Creative confidence: Unleashing the creative potential within us all.* Redfern, Australia: Currency Press.

Lineberry, H. S. & Wiek, A. (2016). Art and sustainability. In *Sustainability science* (pp. 311–324). Dordrecht, NL: Springer.

Magnano, P., Craparo, G., & Paolillo, A. (2016). Resilience and emotional intelligence: Which role in achievement motivation. *International Journal of Psychological Research, 9*(1), 9–20.

Margulis, L. & Sagan, D. (1986). *Microcosmos.* New York, NY: Summit.

Mayer, J. D. (2008). Human abilities: Emotional intelligence. *Annual Review of Psychology, 59,* 507–536. doi:10.1146/annurev.psych.59.103006.093646.

McGuire-Kishebakabaykwe, P. D. (2010). Exploring resilience and indigenous ways of knowing. *Pimatisiwin: A Journal of Aboriginal and Indigenous Community Health, 8,* 117.

Morgan, H. (1996). An analysis of Gardner's theory of multiple intelligence. *Roeper Review, 18*(4), 263–269.

Mulrooney, M. (2012). *Continuity or Collapse? Diachronic Settlement and Land Use in Hanga Hoonu, Rapa Nui (Easter Island)* (Doctoral dissertation), ResearchSpace, Auckland.

Nemeth, D. G., & Olivier, T. W. (2017). *Innovative approaches to individual and community resilience: From theory to practice.* New York, NY: Elsevier Academic Press.

Ngah, R., Abd Wahab, I., & Salleh, Z. (2015). The sustainable competitive advantage of small and medium enterprises (SMEs) with intellectual capital, knowledge management and innovative intelligence: Building a conceptual framework. *Advanced Science Letters, 21*(5), 1325–1328.

Olivier, (2017). *Community resilience, innovative approaches to individual and community resilience* (pp. 59–76). London, UK: Elsevier.

Peariso, J. F. (2008). Multiple intelligences or multiply misleading: The critic's view of the multiple intelligences theory. *Online submission*.

Peiser, B. (2005). From genocide to ecocide: The rape of Rapa Nui. *Energy & Environment*, *16*(3–4), 513–539.

Rival, L. (2009). The resilience of indigenous intelligence. In: *The question of resilience. Social responses to climate change*, (pp. 293–313). Copenhagen, Denmark: The Royal Danish Academy of Science and Letters.

Rotarangi, S. & Russell, D. (2009). Social-ecological resilience thinking: Can indigenous culture guide environmental management? *Journal of the Royal Society of New Zealand*, *39*(4), 209–213. doi:10.1080/03014220909510582.

Shrivastava, P. (2010). Pedagogy of passion for sustainability. *Academy of Management Learning and Education*, *9*(3), 443–455.

Shrivastava, P., Ivanaj, V., & Ivanaj, S. (2012). Sustainable development and the arts. *International Journal of Technology Management*, *60*(1–2), 23–43.

Sinclair, M. (2010). Misconceptions about intuition. *Psychological Inquiry*, 21(4), 378–386.

Sinclair, M., ed. (2014). *Handbook of research methods on intuition*. Cheltenham, UK: Edward Elgar Publishing.

Wesley-Esquimaux, C. C. (2009). Trauma to resilience: Notes on decolonization. In G. G. Valaskakis, M. Dion Stout, & E. Guimond (Eds.), *Restoring the balance: First nation women, community and culture*. Winnipeg, MB: University of Manitoba Press.

Yang, C., Ivanova, E., & Hufnagel, J. (2019). Using contemplative photography in sustainability management education: Pedagogical applications in the United States, Russia, and Germany. Paper presented at the Academy of Management Specialized Conference "Responsible Leadership in Rising Economies", Bled, Slovenia.

9 Principle number 8

Reflection

Definition

Reflective practices help to pause and ponder the situation and its implications before jumping into action.

Teaching Goal

Students practice slowing down, exchanging their automatic responses for thoughtful pauses in order to get in touch with more profound insights.

Meta Goal

To notice one's personal speed and develop comfort in pausing and more patiently exploring issues for a greater understanding of complexity.

Origins of the Principle

One of the surprising findings in my research that launched the idea of a specific sustainability mindset was that the individuals interviewed showed an unusual level of comfort with slowing down and switching from an action-oriented-mode to a reflective mode. Certainly, this would not happen when they were in the midst of a crisis that required urgency, but rather in other moments, when instead of remaining caught up in the expected fast pace of transactions, they carved out some time to reflect. They practiced introspection in different settings: Some took a walk in Nature, others wrote down their thoughts, and others simply sat in silence. In those moments, they sought to step "to the balcony" to get a different perspective.

When we reflect, we thoughtfully ponder an experience to attain greater meaning and learn from a given situation. While we are spontaneously connecting causes and effects, wondering "why did this just happen," the fast pace at which we are living becomes the speed at which we ponder those questions; as a result, the connections may be very superficial or fleeting, not leading to real learning moments. American educator John Dewey introduced the concept of reflection in connection with learning and education. In his book, *How We Think* (1910, 1933), he was already observing that depth of response and slowness are intimately connected. To digest impressions and translate them into meaning and ideas, time is needed, he posited and went on to say that the depth of our reflection determines the quality of our thinking.

Dewey described reflection as a deliberate and active process, different from the passive recollection of an event. When we give active and careful consideration to events and our beliefs, we can extract conclusions that are of great learning (Dewey, 1933, p. 118).

Problems and difficult situations that are puzzling or hard to explain are the best opportunities for reflection and learning, which is what makes this Principle so key for the current challenging times, which are definitively problematic. Dewey suggested posing questions exploring why things turned out the way they did and what actions could have led to a different outcome. This is the same approach used in the U.S. Army, called an After Action Review; part of Army training includes reflecting on what happened, exploring cause-effect linkages, and determining how what happened differed from what was anticipated or expected, and what could be done differently (Meliza et al, 2007).

The power of slowing down to intentionally reflect has been conceptualized and further expanded in different learning models. David Schön (1983, 2017) observed that reflection can help uncover the tacit knowledge that individuals have so that this knowledge can be consciously integrated into their actions. Argyris and Schön (1974) developed the concepts of espoused theories (or values) versus theories in action, signaling the gap between what we believe and what values we actually express through our actions. Reflection is the process that can help individuals become aware of this gap, which may lead to revised behaviors. This is an important step in the development of a Sustainability Mindset, since as long as there is no awareness of this gap, change is unlikely.

David Kolb (1984) created a four-phase learning cycle model, based on the link between an event and the pause to reflect upon it. Pedler, Burgoyne, & Boydell (2001) simplified the terminology of Kolb's model, referring to "*Something happened, What happened? So what? What now?*" Another model (Rimanoczy, 2004) that guides the reflective process toward learning from an action includes the personal contribution and the motivation to act: 1) The feedback we receive from an event: *What happened? How was this different from what we expected?* 2) Awareness of our role in the results: *How did I contribute?* 3) Motivation or need: *Do I feel the need to do something?* 4) Plan: *What will I do?* Reflection is the cognitive process that moves the individual from one step to the next, however, depending on the answers to the questions, the cycle can stop at any step and no learning or action may ensue (see Figure 9.1).

Questions are very powerful tools for educators to prompt reflection and help individuals move along their learning journey. Jack Mezirow (1998) built upon Dewey's work on reflection, suggesting that critical reflection is the primary objective of adult education and also a path for transformative learning experiences. For Mezirow (1997), life provides us with "disorienting dilemmas," which are situations in which we feel perplexed or puzzled by

Figure 9.1 The change cycle

Source: Rimanoczy, 2004.

events that disconfirm our beliefs or the ways in which we make meaning. A situation can challenge our assumptions and paradigms, as long as we allow questioning—which emerges from reflecting on the situation—to happen. This approach can, thus, lead to profound transformative experiences that change how we see ourselves and how we conduct ourselves. TED talks are filled with stories of transformative experiences that changed the course of action of individuals, many of them related to shifts toward sustainability actions or causes.

Scholars have long been exploring the value of transformative learning pedagogies in sustainability education (Brunnquell & Brunstein, 2018; Brunstein, Sambiase, Kerr, Brunnquell, & Perera, 2019; Iyer-Raniga & Andamon, 2016; Moore, 2005; Thomas, 2009). Brookfield (1995) identified the following processes as being central to learning how to be critically reflective: Assumption analysis, contextual awareness, imaginative speculation, and reflective skepticism. Each of these processes is absolutely relevant in developing a mindset shift toward sustainability: When we scrutinize our *assumptions,* we begin to uncover our unseen paradigms; when we explore the *context,* we gain insight into the complexity of the challenges; when we engage our *imagination,* we can envision possibilities and impacts into the future; and when we embed a *skeptic reflective habit,* we may take more conscious decisions.

Why do we need this Principle?

Indisputably, we are living in high-speed times. Even while some educators may have grown up in a slower-paced time, the students populating their classrooms are synchronized to a different velocity. Their attention spans are briefer and, therefore, they are more at ease multitasking than focusing on one topic at a time. This entails a more superficial treatment of the topics, and as we observed in the previous section, lower quality of conclusions and learning. They may be more comfortable in action—"doing," as opposed to the more sedentary reflecting since the former provides a sense of forward movement or progress. Automatic behaviors facilitate attending to many things simultaneously with minimal attention.

Yet automatic behaviors are the opposite of thoughtful actions. And this is precisely what got us into trouble.

As we have been describing in the preceding Principles, much of the unsustainable mindset that created the problems we are facing is due to myopia—an inability to see *long-term* impacts and *interconnections.* We act rapidly and, thus, we fail to appreciate the *complexity* of issues. We jump from assumptions to blaming others, and we miss noticing our *personal contribution* to problems. We are blind to our own assumptions, taking them for "the way things are" and, thus, losing perspective of how things are seen from the other side. We become disconnected from others and miss the broader picture that diversity can bring us. We hold values dear, but rarely stop to explore if our actions are a true expression of those values, or if there is an inconsistency. We ground our identity on values that, in fact, may be at the foundation of unsustainability such as the value of independence, autonomy, competition, wealth, comfort, and speed (Rimanoczy, 2017). And then—something like the Coronavirus happens and forces us all to slow down and suspend our daily routines. With games, parks, sports, eating out, shopping, traveling, and entertaining halted, we found ourselves with time on our hands to reallocate. This forced halt in our hectic rhythm was for many around the globe an unexpected trigger to reflect on how we are living our life and to revise our priorities and habits.

But not all the insights sprouting in times of crisis stay and get embedded into our behavior. Given the importance of our unsustainable habits, what if there was one process to facilitate the rewiring of them? While many of the Principles are interconnected, there is one that has a connection with each of the other 11 Principles (see Figure VI.1 in Part VI). Reflection is that process and it may be less difficult than it seems.

How is this Principle effectively brought into the classroom?

This Principle is translated into the following **Teaching Goal:**

> *Students practice slowing down, exchanging their automatic responses for thoughtful pauses in order to get in touch with more profound insights.*

The long-term aspiration of this Principle is best stated in the **Meta Goal:**

> *To notice one's personal speed and develop comfort in pausing and more patiently exploring issues for a greater understanding of complexity.*

A fast pace is not the only characteristic of the current-day classroom. Technology and access to information is another key trait of our times and has changed how people learn and what they know.

Today's access to knowledge is vastly democratized: With a cell phone and the Internet, we can browse centuries of academic papers in Google Scholar and learn from the brightest across the globe watching them speak at conferences. Wikipedia has replaced the costly Encyclopedia Britannica that only the privileged could buy (and it is more updated). And typing "how do I ...." followed by almost anything will bring up videos and free tutorials to select from. Teilhard de Chardin described the noosphere in 1922, a sphere of thought encircling the Earth that emerged through evolution and as a result of human growth in complexity/consciousness. That is the closest to imagining the Internet, forty years before it was conceived and close to eighty before it was populated with endless contents.

Now, in this context, what do educators bring to the classroom? Certainly not information, since any Google search will bring more updated, varied, and (most times) accurate information. Educators may still see themselves as expert providers of know-how, but is that the real value they are bringing? I recall a conversation with a colleague on how to embed aspects of the Sustainability Mindset into her syllabus. Impossible, she said. I have already so much to content to cover that I cannot include one more thing!

Interestingly, competencies across higher education are frequently listing "critical thinking" as a key goal, yet to drop traditional contents from a syllabus seems very challenging. At the 2020 International Conference of the Academy of Management, Ken Sagendorf, Professor and Director of the Innovation Center at the Anderson College of Business and Computing, Regis University, Colorado, reflected that while faculty focuses mostly on imparting knowledge, a little on developing skills, and minimally on attitudes and mindsets, employers are mostly interested in attitudes and mindsets, somewhat on skills, and minimally on knowledge.

This is why the development of a Sustainability Mindset with students goes in tandem with the mindset of educators themselves. Playing the role of a learning facilitator, stepping temporarily away from the traditional instructor role, is a new way to bring value to our students—a role that requires us to expand our consciousness by exploring our own values, habits of mind, anchors of our identity, and pace. Promoting reflective practices may indeed prompt more transformational learning than exclusive lecturing on contents.

Key components

The key components in this Principle are as follows:

- *Speed as a precious value of our civilization;*
- *Reflection is developed experientially.*

Being such a powerful path for learning and development, the Principle of Reflection has surprisingly few components for its implementation. Compared with the teaching of other Principles—like Ecoliteracy, for example, which covers many different topics, including water, soil, air, waste, social aspects, natural resources, and climate change—meeting the teaching goals of the Principle of Reflection requires educators to lecture less and practice their learning facilitator role more.

We mentioned before that certain values of our culture, highly praised as they may be, are also at the root of our collective unsustainability. In Chapter 7, to fully understand the Principle "Interconnectedness," we suggested addressing the values of autonomy and independence, so important to many of us.

Here the value to address is *speed*. Speed is related to getting things done quickly, covering many topics in less time, and making us feel that we are making progress. It is also associated with being first and being faster than the competitors or at least avoiding lagging behind. What are the downsides of speed, however? What are we missing in depth, in understanding, in seeing the fuller picture? How does speed help (or hurt) efficiency? What may be the illusion of speed? These are some of the angles that can be explored with students through conversations or essays. The benefits of a group discussion are that individuals get to hear different perspectives, and this social learning enriches and multiplies the experience. Written essays may go deeper, and the social learning can be created by assigning peers to read and comment on each other's reflective essays. Some professors ask students to create a blog, which they use throughout the semester and have been conducive to more insightful posts.

Reflection is a Principle that *is learned experientially*. There is no intellectual content to memorize. Rather, it is through personal experiences that insights about one's own pace are developed, and the habit of pausing becomes slowly embedded through repeated moments of practice. Individuals get to live the impacts and benefits of those pauses, and this becomes the best reinforcement for the new habit.

Preparing yourself for the task

Key questions for the educator:

For self-awareness:

- Notice your own pace and rhythm. How can you model slowing down?
- What gets in the way of you slowing down?
- What content may you drop to make space for this Principle in class?
- How do you feel in the learning facilitator role?
- What can you do to feel better in this role?

To prepare the assignments/activities:

- How can you set the context for the conversation about speed? How could this context be connected to the discipline you are teaching?
- There may be individuals in the group that actually experience slowing down periodically. What can they share with their peers?
- How could you bring the students to explore the impact of the COVID-19 on their pace?

Tips for the educator:

- Consider addressing this Principle first **in a conversation** with the group.
- Understanding **the downsides of speed** can help people develop the sensitivity to identify the impact of speed in their own lives and make space for experimenting with slowing down.
- Students may be accustomed to memorize and cite and, thus, may have to gain confidence in the value of exploring and **expressing their own thoughts**.
- **Journaling and reflective essays** are formats that foster reflection.
- Establish **criteria** for a good reflective essay.
- Sitting in a **circle** fosters more reflective conversations.
- For large groups, set up reflective conversations in **small subgroups**.
- **Music** can transmit quiet energy and help set the atmosphere for reflective dialogs.
- Extroverts talk as they think, introverts need to silently connect to their thoughts. In a group setting, create a few minutes of **silent reflection** to give everyone an equal opportunity to reflect before sharing. Writing down their thoughts helps in organizing them in a linear way.
- To develop practice and the habit, find small opportunities to incorporate this Principle **throughout your course**, not just in one session.

An exercise to try out

The coffee shop exercise

This is a simple and powerful experiential learning activity. Invite the students to go to a coffee shop, by themselves, leaving behind their phones or laptop or any reading materials. The exercise consists of being on their own for 45 minutes in the coffee shop. They can be anywhere they want in the store, as long as they don't engage in conversation with other people. They shouldn't bring any pets with them either. It is an individual exercise, not to be done with others. The instruction is just to be there and to remember that doing nothing is part of the exercise.

After the 45 minutes are over, they can leave, and write a reflective essay about the experience.

The instructions need to be given sparsely, without anticipating details. This is important to make the experience personal and unique for everyone and not conditioned by "should I be feeling relaxed? Anxious? Impatient? Nervous? Sleepy? Bored? Should I observe others? Meditate?"

The purpose of this exercise is to create a setting where the individual is by him- or herself, without the usual entertaining and silence-filling technology. Doing nothing is the only instruction, and this will provide an opportunity to notice different sensations, thoughts, or reactions. The reflective essay for processing the experience is a very important part of this exercise. It will confront each individual with what is specific to them: Impatience, relief, physical sensations, enhanced capacity to observe what surrounds them, etc. The reflective essay will most probably connect their experience with any previous class discussions about speed, technology, and pausing to reflect, therefore, reinforcing the impact.

A story

This story took place at a training facility with a small group of executives from the U.S. Postal Service. They were working together on a complex challenge as part of their leadership development program. Their backgrounds were different: Engineers, IT, finance, and operations. I was supporting them as a Learning Coach to provide them with just-in-time team processes or intervening questions. Part of the program included alternating between action (teamwork) and reflection, to extract learnings and to give them a chance to pause to ponder how they felt they were doing, what they could do differently, and what they were learning about working with others and about themselves. But the tendency of the participants was definitely not reflection: They were leaders of action, used to speedy decisions and numerous obligations to attend to in their day-to-day. Although they agreed to participate in the program, the moments of reflection were unwelcome and received as interruptions to their work. So I decided to create a special space, a physical space at one end of the meeting room, where I placed seven chairs in a circle. I called this Our Reflective Corner. Whenever the moment came to create the pause, I invited them to move to our Reflective Corner. The concrete, physical movement to another location made it easier for them to transition from the "active" work to the reflective stance. It helped them accept and integrate those "different" moments as part of their activity and created a positive disposition toward a different tone of sharing and talking: Nothing about work had to be solved or decided. This was like a "break" time, and yet it was still about them—that is, it was no longer viewed as an interruption taking them away from what they wanted or needed to do. They could also make fun of the movement, but no longer in a cynical or passive-aggressive way. It allowed them to be playful, which, in turn, enriched their exchanges. At some point, one of the participants even suggested, "I think it's time to go to our Corner!"

This story shows the importance of creating a special context for reflection; in this case, by moving from one place to another, individuals brought different parts of themselves to the conversation. The most insightful and authentic conversations with students of Al Akhawayn University, Morocco, happened when we went outside and sat together on the lawn.

Other resources

TED Talk by David Peabody – The Art of Reflection https://www.ted.com/talks/david_peabody_the_art_of_reflection?utm_campaign=tedspread&utm_medium=referral&utm_source=ted comshare

TED Talk by James Schmidt, University of Glasgow – The value of self-reflection https://youtu.be/G1bgdwC_m-Y

TED Talk by Daniel Rubin, Tel-Aviv Israel – The power of rest and reflection. About the fast pace living and the need to pause and reflect, inspired by the Shabbat in the Jewish tradition. https://youtu.be/G1bgdwC_m-Y

TED Talk by Ali Fenwick, Hult Ashridge UK - A Reflective Mindset – The Secret to a Better and Longer Life https://youtu.be/YM1yPq0Q_MM

References

Argyris, C. & Schön, D. (1974). *Theory in practice: Increasing professional effectiveness*. San Francisco, CA: Jossey-Bass.

Brookfield, S. (1995). *Becoming a critically reflective teacher*. San Francisco, CA: Jossey-Bass.

Brunnquell, C. & Brunstein, J. (2018). Sustainability in management education: Contributions from critical reflection and transformative learning. *Metropolitan Universities*, *29*(3).

Brunstein, J., Sambiase, M. F., Kerr, R. B., Brunnquell, C., & Perera, L. C. J. (2019). Sustainability in finance teaching: Evaluating levels of reflection and transformative learning. *Social Responsibility Journal*, *16*(2), 179–197.

Dewey, J. (1933). *How we think: A restatement of the relation of reflective thinking to the educative process (1910)*, revised edition. Boston, IL: Heath.

Iyer-Raniga, U. & Andamon, M. M. (2016). Transformative learning: Innovating sustainability education in built environment. *International Journal of Sustainability in Higher Education*. *17*; 1055–122.

Kolb, D. A. (1984). *Experiential learning: Experience as the source of learning and development* (Vol. 1). Englewood Cliffs, NJ: Prentice-Hall.

Meliza, L. L., Goldberg, S. L., & Lampton, D. R. (2007). *After action review in simulation-based training.* Orlando, FL: Army Research Institute for the Behavioral and Social Sciences.

Mezirow, J. (1997). Transformative learning: Theory to practice. *New Directions for Adult and Continuing Education, 1997*(74), 5–12.

Mezirow, J. (1998). On critical reflection. *Adult Education Quarterly, 48*(3), 185–198.

Moore, J. (2005). Is higher education ready for transformative learning? A question explored in the study of sustainability. *Journal of Transformative Education, 3*(1), 76–91.

Pedler, M., Burgoyne, J., & Boydell, T. (2001). *A manager's guide to self-development* (4th edn.), Maidenhead, UK: McGraw-Hill.

Thomas, I. (2009). Critical thinking, transformative learning, sustainable education, and problem-based learning in universities. *Journal of Transformative Education, 7*(3), 245–264.

Rimanoczy, I. (2004). The learning cycle: Steps in the process of learning and change. *Action Learning News*, IFAL.

Rimanoczy, I. (2017). *Big bang being: Developing the sustainability mindset.* London: Routledge.

Schön, D. A. (1983, 2017). *The reflective practitioner: How professionals think in action.* London: Routledge.

10 Principle number 9

Self-awareness

Definition

When we explore our personal values, beliefs, assumptions, and motivations, we gain greater control over our own actions and can see new alternative behaviors.

Teaching Goal

Students experience the power of introspection and scrutinizing the anchors of their identity, and the alignment of their behavior with their espoused values.

Meta Goal

To recognize the aspects of our paradigm that are anchoring us in unsustainability and develop new alternatives that align personal values with the greater good, resulting in new identity anchors.

Origins of the Principle

"Know Thyself" is the translation of the aphorism sculpted in the 4th century BC in the entrance of the Apollo temple in the Greek city of Delphi. The importance of understanding self has been observed throughout history. Philosopher John Locke in 1689 wrote the first elaborations about consciousness, linking them to self-awareness in his *Essay Concerning Human Understanding*.

Philosopher William James, in 1890, considered the father of American psychology, described the role of introspection in developing self-awareness (James, Burkhardt, Bowers, &

Skrupskelis, 1890, 1983). In behavioral sciences, expanding self-awareness became the cornerstone of therapeutic
applications: What we discover about our own motives
and feelings opens up new possibilities of acting. Instead of
being played by our unconscious beliefs and motivations,
we are capable of pondering alternatives. Csikszentmihalyi
(1993, p. 69) points out that "knowing the origin of [our]
motives and becoming aware of our biases is the prerequisite for freedom." This includes the values of the culture
and society into which we are born.

Self-awareness has also been a focus of educational scholarship for a long time. American educator John Dewey suggested that the very purpose of education was to develop
students' self-awareness, something elaborated on by many
other researchers of adult learning. Freire, Argyris, Schön,
Mezirow, Brookfield, and Cranton, among others, have
studied how unconscious paradigms and assumptions come
into play in our behaviors. They stress that the expansion
of self-awareness is a crucial goal of education, particularly
for adult learners.

In organizational settings, Peter Senge called "personal
mastery," meaning a deep understanding of self, one of the
five key disciplines that can create a learning organization.
Kegan and Lahey, in similar ways, addressed the importance of uncovering the tacit assumptions that guide our
behaviors, so that awareness can help to drive behavioral
change. Self-awareness stands as a core content for leadership development programs (Kegan & Lahey, 2001; 2009;
Reams, 2016). In the Change Cycle presented in chapter 9,
self-awareness will help individuals extract meaning from a
given event, explore how they may have contributed to it,
and if they feel the need to change, open up new behaviors.

In connection with sustainability, Stanford scholars
Ehrlich and Kennedy (2005) note that "the collective
actions of individuals lie at the heart of the [environmen-
tal] dilemma" and that "analysis of individual motives and
values should be critical to the solution." Yale professor

James G. Speth (2009) equally notes that among the unseen underlying drivers of our environmental deterioration lie "the values that shape our behavior and determine what we consider important in life." The late writer and former president of Czechoslovakia, Vaclav Havel (1998, p. 30) suggested that a change in the sphere of human conscience is what could change the direction of today's civilization. Similarly, the rich contributions of members of pioneering think tanks such as the Club of Rome and the Tellus Institute have long been ringing the bell about addressing the values that lie at the core of our problems (Laszlo, 1989; Raskin et al, 2002).

Consciousness for Locke meant recognizing oneself, and only after doing so could any moral responsibility be attributed to an individual. Many people today are aware of global issues, such as the state of environmental degradation or social injustice. However, not many see how their own actions can make them unintentional contributors to these types of problems. The excuse of "I didn't know" doesn't help. This sad reality makes the development of self-awareness more urgent than ever.

Why do we need this Principle?

Although self-awareness is a broad term used differently as a learning principle or as a therapeutic goal, we will focus on one particular dimension in the development of a Sustainability Mindset.

In the previous section, we heard several voices connecting environmental deterioration or larger planetary challenges with the values of our shared culture. We need to explore the self-awareness dimensions of values, beliefs, and assumptions that anchor us in unsustainability, particularly how one's individual sense of identity is tied to those dimensions.

Behavioral scientists know that when individuals are able to ponder the motivations and anchors of identity behind their automatic actions, they step into the transformational territory. With a new look at themselves, they can begin to uncover the values, beliefs, and assumptions that may explain dysfunctional behavior. In particular, we all subscribe to certain values, but under closer scrutiny, we may realize that our behaviors are not aligned with the values we espouse. This creates "cognitive dissonance," a state of tension within ourselves that is uncomfortable. The discomfort may cause rationalization or denial, or it can become the fuel to act as we spontaneously seek ways of lowering that tension. As a result, individuals can realize that they always have choices, and this moves them along the change cycle.

Inviting students to pay deliberate attention to themselves, as opposed to focusing on "themes and external issues," can lead to some surprises (for them). Interestingly, studies of key educational experiences among higher education students list self-discovery and identity-questioning as central components of the most memorable experiences (Yair, 2008). In my own experience and the experience of my colleagues at the PRME Working Group on the Sustainability Mindset, higher education students are often initially hesitant to engage in activities different from the routine. Students may not at all expect to have activities such as meditation, dialogs in a circle, reflective essays, or other introspective activities in a seemingly traditional course. However, they can come to regard these activities as a unique opportunity for their own personal development. Understanding self becomes more interesting than theories or technical competencies, particularly when educators can show the link between expanding self-awareness and relating better to others. The benefit of expanding self-awareness, particularly in exploring the anchors of our identity, can help people develop more authenticity and even more understanding and acceptance of diverse others. All these are key aspects of mindset necessary to shape a better world.

How is this Principle effectively brought into the classroom?

This Principle is translated into the following **Teaching Goal:**

> *Students experience the power of introspection and scrutinizing the anchors of their identity and the alignment of their behavior with their espoused values.*

The long-term aspiration of this Principle is best stated in the **Meta Goal:**

> *To recognize the aspects of our paradigm that are anchoring us in unsustainability and develop new alternatives that align personal values with the greater good, resulting in new identity anchors.*

As indicated before, this Principle will open a path of discovery with direct application in the life of every person. Such a path is unusual in higher education but more common in corporate leadership programs. Since the declaration of the Decade of Education for Sustainable Development,[1] many scholars have explored the competencies needed to educate for sustainability, especially how to engage students in appropriate action (Fabricatore & López, 2012; Wiek, Withycombe, & Redman, 2011). Many of the approaches focus on knowledge and thinking competencies aimed at solving complex problems, which is an appropriate approach for *adaptive* actions. However, if we want to engender *preventive* actions, rather than simply reduce unsustainable behaviors, a mindset shift is critical. This represents a whole new level of challenge for educators.

The challenge arises because behaviors are the visible manifestation of tacit beliefs, values, assumptions, and shared paradigms, something that is not automatically corrected via knowledge and problem-solving competencies. John Miller (2007), a pioneer in holistic curriculums, observed that we are living in times of increasing fragmentation, keeping information in silos that don't necessarily connect. In other words, intellectual knowledge may often exist separately from personal values and unspoken assumptions.

Educators need to deal with this gap between head and heart, which stands as the foundation of this book. Shifting a person's mindset may be simpler than imagined (Hermes & Rimanoczy, 2018). In the next section, we will introduce the key components of this Principle and how introspective habits can be brought into the classroom, particularly to help students explore their values and the unsustainable anchors of their identity. The meta goal, which is not expected to be reached by everyone in the short time of a course, is that individuals have transformative experiences and develop new ways of seeing themselves.

Key components

The key components in this Principle are as follows:

*   *Space and time to reflect*
*   *Values of our culture*
*   *Paradigm we live in*
*   *Espoused values and values in action*

The first key component is creating *spaces* and *time for students to reflect*. This may sound obvious, but educators do not always attend to the different learning styles of introverts and extraverts, or students who absorb material at different rates. Some students just are easily distracted or face challenges in understanding the language. Asking a question in class prompts answers and not necessarily reflection. Real reflection requires particular circumstances: A minute of silence and an openness to listen, as well as the curiosity to explore the answers and challenge superficial statements. Asking students to write their reflections helps them refine their thoughts as they convert them into sentences. Time constraints can be managed by having students share their reflections in pairs or trios. If time permits, students can then selectively share what they gleaned from sharing and hearing others' insights. Written assignments and other techniques based on reflection can produce much deeper learning than a literature review or a case study of someone else's situation.

The values of our culture are a central component of this Principle. It is almost impossible to immediately identify what are the values that shape one's identity. However, providing a list of socially accepted values of our culture leads to more introspective moments (Rimanoczy, 2017, p 98). The educator can prepare her or his own list and ask students to add their own. Here are some of the suggested values to discuss:

- Achievement: This may be associated with the importance of personal or professional success, the idea of being a winner (not a loser), expectations (of self and others), and perceived importance of effort, talent, persistence, fame, respectability, etc.
- Economic growth: Value placed on GDP, linear models, and corporate quarterly goals.
- Wealth: Financial wellbeing, material possessions, and symbols of wealth.
- Competition: Motivation to win, to improve oneself, to try harder, and to outperform others.
- Independence and autonomy: Self-reliance, self-empowerment, freedom, self-sufficiency, resourcefulness, and control of circumstances.
- Control: Empowerment of self, being in charge oneself, having good plans or measurements, anticipating situations, not being taken by surprise or being unprepared, and having a sense of certainty.
- Comfort: Ease, efficiency, better standards or conditions of living, more fun, less hardship.
- Speed: Covering more topics, doing more in less time, arriving sooner, being first and not being left behind, and being a pioneer or champion.

- Knowledge: Being informed and up to date, showing understanding and mastery, doing informed advocacy, and being respected, cited, and influential.
- The right to have a family is a socially accepted value, which is also at the core of many of our planetary challenges. Educators may not feel comfortable addressing this very deeply held value, which has also religious connotations in many cultures.

A discussion about socially accepted values will make visible the tacit *paradigm* we live in and which undergirds our behaviors and choices.

The list of the positive aspects of such values can be constructed collectively with the students, for a partic-ipative engagement. Then the downside of each value needs to be explored. It is possible that students by themselves start to name some downsides when listing the positives. Completing a fuller picture of the positive and less obvious negative implications of the socially accepted values will provide an understanding of one's own values.

This may lead to the exploration of our *espoused values* (the values we adhere to, we hold dearly) versus our *values in action* (those that are actually expressed through our behav-iors and are not always consistent with those espoused)—a key introspective activity to implement this Principle of Self-Awareness (Argyris & Schön, 1974).

Preparing yourself for the task

Key questions for the educator:

For self-awareness:

- What are the anchors of my identity?
- Why am I doing what I am doing?
- What are my personal paradoxes?

To prepare the assignments/activities:

- What are your expectations about the possible reactions and responses of the students? Suspend expectations and keep your judgments to yourself.
- How ready do you think the audience is for this Principle? When would be the best timing to introduce it?
- What activities do you think would be most powerful given the characteristics of the audience?
- How does this Principle connect with the discipline you are teaching? Establish those connections first before seeking activities.

Tips for the educator:

- **Create a non-judgmental setting:** The anchors of our identity are a very sensitive area. Particularly if we are not conscious of them or their implications, we may not see values as "something I have" but as a more permanent "who I am." This can bring emotional reactions and the need to defend ourselves. As a result, it is important that the facilitator doesn't judge or suggest which are right or wrong values. Think of this as a scientific exploration of values. They are what they are, and mostly they are adopted without much thought given to their downsides. Certainly, there may be no conscious link with the way in which those dearly held cultural values have largely brought us to the problems the world is facing today. This demonstrates how powerful this Principle is.
- **It's about asking questions, not about providing answers:** Educators are commonly trained as experts to provide answers, to guide and transfer their knowledge or expertise. This Principle, however, calls for a learning facilitator or even a coaching role. The power will be in asking questions, or in students asking questions. Instructors should not provide the answers. All

learners have to find their own answers in matters of identity. The instructor provides a safe space to begin developing this Principle. Wear your "coach hat," not your "instructor hat," when dealing with this Principle.

* **Create introspective assignments:** Reflective essays, dialogs in a circle, and exercises in trios or small groups are options that foster self-discovery. Clearly establish the criteria for the essays, since there are no right-wrong statements. Place higher value on deeper, more engaged treatments of the questions. We must remember, though, that not every student is ready to explore at the same depth. This is just part of their journey.

* **Exploring personal values is definitely personal:** Discussing the values of our shared culture may be more distant and abstract, lending itself to a more intellectual discussion. This changes when the conversation gets into which of these values are personally more important for us. Which ones define who we are? Journaling and discussions in dyads or triads may provide the necessary intimate context to allow this exploration, perhaps without ever sharing the results with the larger group. What counts is the experience of the individual, not how much they are willing to share. Other activities that can provide introspection are those that use art: Visiting an art exhibit, making a collage, or creating a digital portfolio of photos are some powerful choices[2].

An exercise to try out

Gallery walk and talk

This exercise offers students the opportunity to explore and discuss the values of our culture in a creative setting.
   Materials:

* Flip-chart paper;

- Markers in different colors;
- Tape.

Prepare the flip charts by writing on top of one paper one of the identified socially accepted values (see list above). Under the title, draw a vertical line dividing the paper into two columns. On the left column, write, "The good is …." On the Right column, write, "The downsides are…." Prepare one flip chart for each value, or two values on one flip chart, separating the first from the second with a horizontal line.

Place the posters on or alongside the walls of the classroom or hallway if available, sufficiently separate from each other so that students will be able to hear the discussion in their small team (see below). This will become the "Gallery."

Divide the class into small groups of 3–4 students, and introduce the Gallery Walk and Talk: Each group will start at a different flipchart, read and discuss, and write their thoughts on the poster. Then they will move clockwise to read the next poster.

You can allocate between 5 and 7 minutes maximum to each poster. As students move along this Gallery of posters, they will be able to read what others have written, add their own thoughts, and/or question and comment on previous thoughts; the result is a social learning experience. Make sure that when they have finished the round, they all will have had a chance to quickly skim what others have added since they passed by that poster.

Once every team has finished the round and checked out the posters, open a dialog about the experience. This is not a debrief of the process (was it noisy, too long, too short, couldn't read, etc.) nor about the contents (what they wrote on the posters). Guide the dialog instead to the personal implications, with questions such as:

- How did you feel discussing the positives?
- How easy or difficult was it to find the negatives? Why?

- Which aspects did you feel more surprised about?
- Which values are dearer to you?
- What did you think about the negatives of those that are dearer to you?
- What meanings emerged for you?

An alternative is to wrap up with a process or content debrief and ask them to address the personal meaning questions in a reflective essay.

A story

At an MBA class, we used the Gallery Walk and Talk exercise, ending it with a dialog to share reflections and insights and to extract meaning. The room was set up with a large circle of chairs, where students could sit comfortably and see everyone. There was no obligation to speak, and students could participate by listening or by talking. One of the rules of the dialog was to suspend judgments and avoid ping-pong interactions. This was a space to listen to each other, not to convince anyone to change her or his opinion.

The conversation started with highlights of some of the negative characteristics of the values and also questioning if the positives actually didn't compensate for the downsides. Some students couldn't find any negatives to some values and were surprised when others listed some. We explored where those values originated, how important they were for all of us, and which ones were more important personally. Some talked about some "AHA!" moments as they listed the downsides and reflected on how "to get all the good without the bad." (A polarity to be managed!) One student commented that wealth was an important value, because that was a really good goal. He explained that he was attending school to graduate and get a better salary, so that he could get a car and a house and get married and have a family. As he spoke, he heard himself saying,

"Because if I don't have that, who am I? If you take away all my goals, what is left?"

The questions remained in the air, cushioned by silence. We could hear the pain in his voice in this moment that was reflecting a glimpse into some expanded self-awareness. He started to concede that fulfillment and happiness are human desires, but we tend to base our *whole identity* on those goals. It is a profound insight to realize that there is a self beyond the successful professional, the married person, the happy owner of a home. The realization that we are not what we do, what we own, or what we achieve opens a window into the experience of a higher level of self.

Other resources

What is wealth? How it means something different for everyone. https://www.listenmoneymatters.com/wealthy-definition-of-wealth/

Our finite world. Website with critiques about Globalization. https://ourfiniteworld.com/2013/02/22/twelve-reasons-why-globalization-is-a-huge-problem/

The Story of Solutions. Animated short video from The Story of Stuff that explores how we could design a different way of living, questioning some values including consumption and competition. https://storyofstuff.org/movies/the-story-of-solutions/ Also **The Story of Change** – https://storyofstuff.org/movies/story-of-change/

MAN. Cartoon about the consequences of our anthropocentric paradigm http://www.youtube.com/watch?v=WfGMYdalClU&feature=youtube_gdata_player

The price of materialism. Animated video about our paradigm and consequences. https://www.youtube.com/watch?feature=player_embedded&v=VRcVS4Ql-Pc

Juliet Schor and the **Plenitude Economy** – Video (also her books) https://www.youtube.com/watch?v=HR-YrD_KB0M

The Happy Planet. TED Talk by Nic Marks, reflecting about GDP and happiness https://www.ted.com/talks/nic_marks_the_happy_planet_index?language=en

Notes

1. https://unesdoc.unesco.org/ark:/48223/pf0000141629. United Nations Educational, Scientific and Cultural Organization. (2007). *The UN decade of education for sustainable development (DESD 2005–2014): The first two years.* Paris, France: / UNESCO.
2. See the work of Yang, Ivanova & Hufnagel, 2019 on the use of contemplative photography in sustainability management education.

References

Argyris, C., & Schön, D. A. (1974). *Theory in practice: Increasing professional effectiveness.* San Francisco, CA: Jossey-Bass.

Csikszentmihalyi, M. (1993). *The evolving self: A psychology for the third millennium.* New York, NY: HarperCollins.

Ehrlich, P. & Kennedy, D. (2005). Millennium assessment of human behavior. *Science, 309*, 562–563.

Fabricatore, C. & López, X. (2012). Sustainability learning through gaming: An exploratory study. *Electronic Journal of e-learning, 10*(2), 209–222.

Havel, V. (November–December 1998). Spirit of the earth, *Resurgence*, p 30.

Hermes, J. & Rimanoczy, I. (2018). Deep learning for a sustainability mindset. *The International Journal of Management Education, 16*(3), 460–467.

James, W., Burkhardt, F., Bowers, F., & Skrupskelis, I. K. (1890, 1983). *The principles of psychology* (Vol. 1, No. 2). London: Macmillan.

Kegan, R. & Lahey, L. L. (2001). *Seven languages for transformation: How the way we talk can change the way we work.* San Francisco, CA: Jossey-Bass.

Kegan, R. & Lahey, L. L. (2009). *Immunity to change: How to overcome it and unlock potential in yourself and your organization.* Cambridge, MA: Harvard Business Press.

Laszlo, E. (1989). *The inner limits of mankind: Heretical reflections on today's values, culture and politics.* Columbus, OH: Hallen Assoc.

Locke, J. (1952). 1689. An essay concerning human understanding. https://www.britannica.com/biography/John-Locke/An-Essay-Concerning-Human-Understanding (Retrieved on May 22, 2019).

Miller, J. P.. (2007). *The holistic curriculum* (Vol. 17). Toronto, ON, Canada: University of Toronto press.

Raskin, P., Banuri, T., Gallopin, G., Gutman, P., Hammond, A., Kates, R., & Swart, R. (2002). *Great transition: The promise and lure of the times ahead*. Boston, MA: Stockholm Environmental Institute.

Reams, J. (2016). Immunity to change revisited: Theoretical foundations for awareness based practices for leadership development. *Integral Review, 12*(1), 163–196.

Rimanoczy, I. (2017). *Big bang being: Developing the sustainability mindset*. London: Routledge.

Speth, J. G. (2009). *The bridge at the edge of the world: Capitalism, the environment, and crossing from crisis to sustainability*. New Haven, CN: Yale University Press.

Wiek, A., Withycombe., L., & Redman, C. L. (2011). Key competencies in sustainability: A reference framework for academic program development. *Sustainability Science, 6*(2), 203–218.

Yair, G. (2008). Key educational experiences and self-discovery in higher education. *Teaching and Teacher Education, 24*(1), 92–103.

Yang, C., Ivanova, E., & Hufnagel, J. (2019). Using contemplative photography in sustainability management education: Pedagogical applications in the United States, Russia, and Germany. Paper presented at the Academy of Management Specialized Conference "Responsible Leadership in Rising Economies", Bled, Slovenia.

Part V

Spiritual Intelligence

We are now entering the last content area: Spiritual Intelligence. This is the most controversial content area in the context of higher education, particularly in the Western world. In the Orient, religions are seen to support spirituality and are more integrated with institutions and the workplace (Purushothaman, 2014). But in the Occidental world, spirituality is associated with religion, a topic that, in most educational institutions, is intentionally avoided because spirituality and religion are seen as pertaining to the realm of the individual. The exceptions are theological studies and institutions within a particular religious tradition that consider religion part of the curriculum.

But religion and spirituality are not synonymous. There are many definitions of Spiritual Intelligence covering a variety of elements, from spontaneity to compassion (King & DeCicco, 2009; Zohar, 2012). Establishing this as a content area was a way of organizing components of the Sustainability Mindset identified in my research (Rimanoczy, 2010). In this context, I define spirituality as "thoughts that people have about being connected to a higher order, and the consequences of this connection on one's life and behavior, such as the need to find purpose, make a contribution, or commit to actions for the greater good of our society" (Rimanoczy, 2017, p. 26). This is aligned with King and DeCicco's version of Spiritual

Intelligence as including the abilities to critically contemplate the nature of existence, derive personal meaning and purpose, be aware of self and others' transcendence, and enter higher states of consciousness. The spiritual orientation to Nature and business has shaped our paradigms in different cultural traditions (Zsolnai, 2014).

Thus, in this section, we will introduce the final three Principles, placed in the content area of Spiritual Intelligence: Purpose, Oneness with Nature, and Mindfulness.

References

King, D. B. & DeCicco, T. L. (2009). A viable model and self-report measure of spiritual intelligence. Transpersonal Studies, *28*, 68–85.

Purushothaman, K. (2014). *Workplace spirituality: profile and influence of spiritually-inspired business leaders-a cross cultural perspective* (Doctoral dissertation). Monash University.

Rimanoczy, I. (2017). Big bang being: Developing the sustainability mindset. London: Routledge.

Rimanoczy, I. B. (2010). Business leaders committing to and fostering sustainability initiatives (Doctoral dissertation). Teachers College, Columbia University.

Zohar, D. (2012). Spiritual intelligence: The ultimate intelligence. New York, NY: Bloomsbury Publishing.

Zsolnai, L. (Ed.). (2014). The spiritual dimension of business ethics and sustainability management. Berlin, Germany: Springer.

11 Principle number 10

Purpose

Definition
Defining our purpose provides an unconscious compass, and when it is grounded in values of our higher self, we actively shape a better world.

Teaching Goal
Students identify something that they feel passionate about through which they can make a difference for the greater good.

Meta Goal
One successful experience of making a difference provides deep satisfaction, a spiritual "high" that creates an unconscious desire to replicate it.

Origins of the Principle

As part of my research, I studied the literature related to individuals engaging in altruistic actions or actions for the greater good, which I related to individuals championing sustainability initiatives. Some of the aspects indicated in the literature were: The sense of a personal mission; the desire or need to make a difference; and the desire or need to have a more meaningful or purposeful life (Bolles, 1991; Kovan & Dirkx, 2003; Kroth & Boverie, 2000; Rehm, 1990).

Although I was not expecting to find spiritual motivation amongst the business leaders of my study, spirituality was cited in the literature as a factor in the motivations of people acting for the common good, associated with questions like *Who am I?* (identity) and *Why am I here?* (purpose) (Kroth & Boverie, 2000; Leider, 2015; Neal, 2008; Stephan, 1989). A sense of communal responsibility was observed, moving individuals to work for social causes or greater equity (Tisdell, 2003). This has been called "emancipatory spirituality," and can be seen in people focused on transforming the world or dedicated to environmental sustainability (Lerner, 2000).

This relationship can also be found in religious traditions. The Judeo-Christian religion mentions notions of calling, service, and mission; Buddhism offers the concept of "right livelihood" as a work "consciously chosen, done with full awareness and care" (Sinetar, 1987, p. 9). The concept of dharma in the Hindu religion is the place assigned to each person in the world order, where they are best able to fulfill a particular task for the greater good (Erickson, 1969).

The interest in making a difference and living a meaningful life is associated with an "outward looking spirituality" (English, 2000, p. 3): "A spiritual person reaches beyond his or her self ... and assumes responsibility for caring about others" (p 30). In the 1990s, Robert Greenleaf connected his corporate leadership role with his interest in management theories and coined the term "Servant Leadership" to describe the link between service and purpose. Spiritual Intelligence researchers Zohar and Marshall (2000) note that when people use their unique gifts and talents to serve others, they experience a sense of spiritual wholeness. Victor Frankl (1985) described at length the power of purpose in his book, *Man's Search for Meaning*, analyzing his own experience of surviving the Holocaust.

Wong (1998)'s Personal Meaning Profile includes statements related to making a difference, making the world a better place, dedicating oneself to a good cause, making a positive contribution to society, and leaving behind a good and lasting legacy. He uses these statements as indicators of self-transcendence, showing the intimate connection between positive personal feelings and actions for the greater good. A more recent study surveying 322 leaders found that they were driven by a sense of greater purpose and responsibility for others. This ranked second in order of importance (frequency) in the choices of the respondents (Tsao & Laszlo, 2019, p. 131).

Fourteen out of the 16 leaders in my research indicated that a sense of purpose, a personal mission, or the need to make a difference played a strong motivational role in their actions (Rimanoczy, 2010). This led me to explore whether these altruistic motivations were the consequence of some traumatic personal experience, or perhaps linked to aging and life crises. The literature offered multiple studies connecting developmental stages with the idea of life purpose or mission, associating this also with mid-life crisis, mortality awareness, and a simple shift in time availability and priorities, for example, when individuals no longer have work or family commitments (Fraser, 2001). But there are also studies that demonstrate a lifetime exploration of existential questions, purpose, and reasons for being as a characteristic of human beings (Jarvis, 1983; Kroth & Boverie, 2000; Murchú, 1998). To understand whether these factors played a role was important given the aim of my research to identify what educators could develop intentionally as opposed to that which was in the realm of personal, irreproducible events, and experiences.

The findings pointed in two directions. Personal traumatic experiences acted as a trigger for some individuals to revisit their priorities and question their life purpose, in the sense of Mezirow's transformational "disorienting dilemmas." In other cases, it was a slow and incremental journey of expanding awareness and insights, with recurring reflections about their role in their organization, their mission, or what difference they could make. Interestingly, some reflected and wished, in hindsight, that someone had asked them about their purpose earlier in life because that might have prompted more meaningful actions sooner. This had been noted in previous studies exploring whether adult educators could help in the development of personal missions, leading to a finding of the positive potential impact of mentors or educators (Kroth, 1997). When people's attention is brought to the question of purpose, what may have been serendipitous can become intentional, reinforcing actions for the greater good. This has been noted in the Intentional Change Theory, which indicates that setting a clear intention drives behavioral change (Boyatzis & Howard, 2006). For example, Ben Cohen and Jerry Greenfield, cofounders of the ice cream business Ben & Jerry's, were pioneers in terms of corporate social responsibility (CSR), but started their initiatives without much thought: Their goal was to find a way to connect with their community. Once they began to realize how much this was valued by their neighbors and clients, and when they learned about the CSR-pioneering initiatives of Anita Roddick in The Body Shop, their efforts became intentional and more focused. Therein may lie the answer to the next question: Why do we need this Principle?

Why do we need this Principle?

Michigan University professor Andrew Hoffman (2017) clearly connects planetary challenges with the opportunity to make them the core of our purpose. In his book, *Finding Purpose*, he observes how every generation faces a "Great Work" that has to be accomplished, a tacit obligation of sorts to fulfill a role that history imposes on us as we face challenges of notable magnitude. He indicates that the focus of the Great Work of the 21st century should be on the Anthropocene, the name given to the current geologic epoch that recognizes man's negative (and likely irreversible) effect on the Earth's ecosystems. There is much that this generation's "Great Work" can attempt to achieve by focusing on the Anthropocene. The 17 Sustainable Development Goals (SDGs) established in 2015 by the United Nations Global Compact outline in detail the gap between where we are and where we want to be for a world "that works for all," in the words of former UN Secretary General Ban Ki-moon. The SDGs offer a direction that speaks to every individual, every organization, every profession, and state. It has been said that we know what has to be done, and for the first time in human history, we have the technologies to address the problems. Will we do it? Are we doing it fast enough?

The answer is probably not, and this Principle can offer some help. When we are able to connect the personal search for meaning and wholeness, whether secular or religious, with the multiple opportunities to help shape a better world, the cocktail becomes powerful and engaging. Exclusively addressing the minds of students, convincing them with hard data about the many stresses of the planet, may build up their ecoliteracy but it is hardly a motivator in itself. As Nic Marks noted in his TED Talk, Martin Luther King Jr. began his famous speech with the statement, "I have a dream." Would it have been equally inspiring for generations to come, had he started with, "I have a nightmare?" We know the answer, yet there is an overwhelming volume of "nightmare" information coming to us through media, social networks, news, and tweets. This very book began with the Ecoliteracy Principle, aimed at providing a broad and encompassing view of our planetary challenges. Yet this is but one Principle, and the subsequent 11 address how we feel, how we are unintentionally contributing to problems, what and how we think, who we are, who we want to be, and what difference we want to make in the world. The balance between information, feelings, our higher self, and actions needs to be improved or even established in order to capitalize its fueling energy. The Principle of Purpose can offer some valuable guidance.

How is this Principle effectively brought into the classroom?

This Principle is translated into the following **Teaching Goal:**

> *Students identify something that they feel passionate about, through which they can make a difference for the greater good.*

The long-term aspiration of this Principle is best stated in the **Meta Goal:**

> *One successful experience of making a difference provides deep satisfaction, a spiritual "high" that creates an unconscious desire to replicate it.*

We can help students reflect on their purpose or on what difference they would like to make, prompting their thinking in a direction they normally might not go. We know they are busy responding to academic and/or work-related demands, without many opportunities to ponder why they are doing what they are doing, and what contribution they would like to make to the world. Educators agree that the goal of their work is to prepare individuals to act in more effective and responsible ways in the world, independent of their discipline. Yet there is a disconnect between the contents covered and how students apply them, beyond writing up fictional case reports. What about connecting the contents with real-time, real-life application of this knowledge?

The concept of "life purpose or mission" also needs to be demystified and brought into a more manageable context. Finding a small opportunity to make a difference related to the topic we may be teaching is a powerful learning experience. For example, some accounting students decided to apply what they were learning to a volunteer accounting effort. The task was simple and required minimal input from the instructor, yet the advice proved very valuable to the person receiving the accounting advice. Students of the University of Central Florida applied their learnings to a project developing organic vegetable gardens in the backyards of a residential community. The neighbors enjoyed the harvest, and the surplus was taken to a local food pantry. These small-scale, achievable initiatives are multidimensional learning experiences, going far beyond the specific contents of a course. People connecting with social causes learn new skills, develop social sensitivity, clarify their values, and deepen their sense of identity (Boggs, 1986). Furthermore, the accomplishment of modest initiatives that provide service or assistance to others develops a sense of confidence, a much-needed trait in midst of the overwhelming social and environmental challenges surrounding us. The giver' sense of joy vastly exceeds the grateful joy of the receiver, as has been repeatedly observed by students. These types of experiences create a memory of a spiritual "high" that is sought again later, opening the path to more actions for the greater good.

Key components

The key components in this Principle are as follows:

* *Self-reflection on what purpose means for us*;
* *New models of organizing life*;
* *New economic models where business is an agent for world benefit—for example, social enterprises, B corporations, public benefit corporations*; and
* *A real project, small or modest, that makes a difference.*

The central component of this Principle is *self-reflection on the personal meaning of purpose*. This has different responses for everyone and probably also evolving significance as students deepen their reflection. As mentioned in the previous section, it is important to decouple the idea of purpose from grandiose life goals, because the loftier they are, the more utopian, and this defeats the aim of having an achievable goal. What counts is the *process of pondering the idea* of having a purpose and making a difference, much more than stating an ambitious life project. If we think of the different Principles introduced here as "lenses" through which we look unto the world—embedded filters that help us make meaning in sustainable ways—then Purpose can become an open-ended, recurrent inquiry. What is the difference I may make ... today? In this situation? In this context?

Another way to address Purpose is revisiting the values that are expressed through our way of living or in our decisions. This is connected with the exploration of the values of our culture that we described in the previous Principle. If students have difficulties integrating the idea of a purposeful life with the (perhaps contrasting) context in which they live, then examples of new models of organizing life can be helpful. One such example is *Transition Towns*, the international grassroots movement of communities collaborating in reimagining and rebuilding our world (See Resources at the end of this chapter).

Continuing with the introduction of current and existing alternatives, the concept of *business as an agent for world benefit* could be a model of interest for any professional discipline. What is the purpose of business? This question may elicit different answers from physicians, farmers, hospitality professionals, engineers, lawyers, and educators. We all are offering some kind of service, as owners, contractors, or employees. Tracing back in history how services and goods were traded, we may reach the understanding of the social service at the foundation of our exchanges. We are interconnected, as we saw before, and we are collectively helping each other in the community, whether we are aware of it or not. How has this concept evolved, changed, been distorted? What are the implications? As in the previous component, *New models of organizing life*, valuable examples abound these days if students cannot imagine examples of purpose-centered businesses. The Fowler Center for Business as Agent of World Benefit, at Case Western Reserve University in Cleveland, has established the AIM2Flourish initiative, where thousands of examples of businesses from around the world are featured, each with one common characteristic: They are profitable businesses addressing the real needs of the community. Their innovative products and services address one or several of the SDGs, often with the owners not even realizing it. The platform is populated through students, who, with guidance of their professors, identify some businesses in their community that meet the criteria (being profitable and addressing some of the SDGs). Then students interview the owners, write the story, and nominate the business candidate for the yearly Flourish Prizes. This very creative system provides learning opportunities for students as they investigate their own community, for their professors and business leaders interviewed—and also expands beyond to the (nonnominated) competitors, raising the bar. Additionally, all the stories and candidates are featured on the free website, becoming a further resource and inspiration for educators and students.

Other new purpose-driven models can be discussed, such as *social enterprises* (business that serve some social needs, whether for profit or nonprofit), and *Public Benefit Corporations* (available in certain states in the U.S.), a relatively new legal incorporation that allows organizations to identify a purpose beyond maximizing shareholder value. *B Corporations* are organizations certified by B Lab, a nonprofit organization that sets standards for social and environmental performance, accountability, and transparency. There are over 3,200 certified B Corporations in 71 countries, setting new standards of excellence, both for competitors and clients.

Finally, the best avenue to develop this Principle is experiential, fostering the pursuit of a *project* to make a difference, even if it is a modest one. Many institutions are incorporating service learning opportunities.

Preparing yourself for the task

Key questions for the educator:

For self-awareness:

- What is your current purpose? How motivating is it for you?
- If you could do anything, what would you do?
- When you are at your best, what unique talents are you engaging?
- When was the last time that you felt you were making a difference?
- How is making a difference a conscious intention in your life, in your teaching?

To prepare the assignments/activities:

- What is the soonest that you can introduce a real project (see Key Components, above), to balance ecoliteracy-related contents?
- How ready do you think your audience is for this Principle? What would be the best timing for a conversation about this topic?
- How does this Principle connect with the context and with the subject you are teaching this group?

Tips for the educator:

- **Dialogs** about the values of our culture, the role of purpose, and alternative models are soft ways to enter the conversation about this Principle. Students can also be invited to research alternative models.
- Experiential learning through a **project to make a difference** is a rich learning experience. Students can be invited to select an area that they care personally about, and connect it with some natural gifts, talents,

or resources. For example, one student liked to be in Nature, had a kayak, and enjoyed spending time with friends on the water. She organized a kayaking event for families and friends to clean up the Hudson River in New York. It became an educational initiative for all those participating. The students involved in planning the event learned about working and planning in a team, making decisions, and communicating among themselves and with the outside world. They practiced creativity in designing the event. They learned about river pollution, and benchmarks of best processes for water clean-up. They received positive feedback from participants, which provided them self-confidence and reinforced their feelings of agency.

- **Reflective essays and journaling** are useful techniques for prompting introspection and helping students pause and explore this topic. The six Why Exercise, for example, invites student to answer six times why he/she is doing a certain activity that is important or a priority—for example, studying or working. This exercises leads to a more profound exploration of our motivations and may connect to questions related to our higher purpose.[1]
- **Learning Partners** is an easy pedagogical resource to promote reflection and self-exploration with another colleague. Partnerships can be formed at the beginning of the course, rotated periodically, assigned randomly, or left to the students' preference. It should be complemented with periodic reports, questions assigned to discuss, posts, or, if appropriate, dialogs in the larger group.

An exercise to try out

The amazing achievement award

This is a visioning exercise that provides students with a structured and guided format to identify and shape a long-term goal to make a difference—a goal about which they are particularly energized.

Instructions:

This is an exercise in time travel. You are now seven years in the future. It is [date here], and you will receive an Award for some amazing achievement. You will have 30 minutes to write the acceptance speech for the Award. In that speech you will cover the following points:

- What is it that you did to receive this Award (the achievement, accomplishment);
- What were some major milestones in the journey to this day;
- What were some obstacles you encountered and how you overcame them; and
- Who do you want to thank for their support/help.

After the 30 minutes, depending on the size of the group, you can invite all individuals to stand up and read their speech to the class, to read it to each other in duos or small groups, or ask only a few interested volunteers to share their speech.

I have used this exercise many times, adapting it to the context. For example, you can create a special event for the speeches, and record them on videos on their phones. This gives more significance to the activity, and the whole group can be inspired and excited with the diversity of the achievements, celebrating each other in a high-energy and festive atmosphere. The choice of seven years is because it is far enough into the future that anything is possible, yet it is not so far that it is beyond our imagination. The seven-year timeframe makes the dream achievable.

The exercise in itself is a prompt to think about what exciting goals students could set for themselves, and then start imagining the steps that have to happen to achieve those goals. At times the exercise becomes the first step for a real project that is implemented (as in my personal case[2]). The careful design of a goal in our mind creates intentionality, which remains in the preconscious level, influencing our ulterior decisions and choices. It is a well-known coaching technique to invite a person to visualize the achievement of a goal, in all its details: What does it feel like having achieved it? What do you see, smell, hear? Who do you see there, where are you? What are you wearing? Etc. The richness of the details contributes to embedding the goal into our preconscious mind and fuel the intentionality.

A story

A student in an MBA class in New York selected an unusual project: He wanted to grow a cucumber. I challenged him, asking how this project would make him feel proud of himself, what was the difference that he wanted to make, and if this would be something fulfilling. My questions were based on my concern that he might be trying to find an easy way out of the assignment, which would deprive him ultimately from having a meaningful experience. Yet he replied to my questions with different arguments, not hesitating about his choice.

After 14 weeks, as the course was drawing to an end, students had to prepare a presentation about their projects and their learnings along the way. This student came to class with a PowerPoint with photos about himself and the progressive changes of the cucumber plant, leading up to the vegetable he brought to the class. He explained that he discovered that the use of pesticides had dramatically impacted the bee population in his area, and as a consequence, the flowers of his plant were not pollinated. After doing some research, he decided to hand-pollinate them, which was tedious and also unsustainable—although it helped him in this case. He also altered some of his habits, for example, he became preoccupied with weather conditions and rain patterns and stopped going out late because he had to water his plant early in the morning, something his friends joked about. Finally, he reflected how much he had liked this difficult experiment, which reconnected him in a way with his grandfather, who had been a farmer all his life. Studying in Manhattan, he had envisioned a successful career in Wall Street in the financial services sector; however, this project had made him revise his values and preferences. He decided that instead he would set up an organic farm and move upstate. This transformational experience was not something I had anticipated, and neither had he, but it shows the power of incorporating a real project that is meaningful for the student.

Other resources

Free app provided by B Corporation to monitor and plan progress toward the SDGs. https://bcorporation.net/welcome-sdg-action-manager

The free teaching and learning platform featuring profitable businesses serving the SDGs from around the world. www.Aim2Flourish.com

https://transitionnetwork.org/

TED Talk by Rob Hopkins, creator of Totnes Transition Towns, about community involvement in development. https://www.youtube.com/watch?v=1LQMK__-5tk

TED Talk by Rob Hopkins, The story of the Transition Town. https://youtu.be/r3L9n20myqk

Animated cartoon: Do you dare to dream? https://www.youtube.com/watch?v=HhFxQlDPjaY&feature=youtube_gdata_player

Ocean clean up initiative. https://youtu.be/uguRuClIdTw

Inspiring video by the founder of Charitywater organization. https://www.charitywater.org/donate/the-spring?utm_medium=ppc&utm_source=adwords&utm_campaign=brand_paid&gclid=EAIaIQobChMIy6nj-fL35wIViobACh3v0QUzEAAYASAAEgJXQ_D_BwE

Notes

1. For example: Why are you here? Because I need the credits. Why? Because I want to graduate this year. Why? Because I want to get a better job with my degree. Why? Because I want more money. Why? Because I want to have a family, a home. Why? Because I want to be happy...

2. I did a TED Talk about what was, for me, a significant Amazing Achievement Award exercise.

References

Boggs, D. L. (1986). A case study of citizen education and action. *Adult Education Quarterly, 37*(1), 1–13.

Bolles, R. N. (2005). *How to find your mission in life.* Parachute, CO: Parachute Library.

Boyatzis, R., & Howard, A. (2006). Positive and negative emotional attractors and intentional change. *Journal of Management Development. 5*(7):657–670.

English, L. M. (2000). Spiritual dimensions of informal learning. *New Directions for Adult and Continuing Education, 2000*(85), 29–38.

Erickson, E. H. (1969). *Gandhi's truth.* Toronto, ON, Canada: George J. McLeod.

Frankl, V. E. (1985). *Man's search for meaning.* New York, NY: Simon and Schuster.

Fraser, L. A. (2001). *The development of commitment to the common good, the case of adults learning about global issues* (Doctoral dissertation). National Library of Canada= Bibliothèque nationale du Canada.

Hoffman, A. J. (2017). *Finding purpose: Environmental stewardship as a personal calling.* Abingdon, UK: Routledge.

Jarvis, P. (1983). The lifelong religious development of the individual and the place of adult education. *Lifelong Learning: The Adult Years, 6*(9), 20–23.

Kovan, J. T. & Dirkx, J. M. (2003). "Being called awake": The role of transformative learning in the lives of environmental activists. *Adult Education Quarterly, 53*(2), 99–118.

Kroth, M. (1997). Life Mission and Adult Learning. An Exploratory Study Examining Theoretical Relationships and Their Impact upon Adult Education.

Kroth, M. & Boverie, P. (2000). Life mission and adult learning. *Adult Education Quarterly, 50*(2), 134–149.

Leider, R. J. (2015). *The power of purpose: Creating meaning in your life and work.* Berrett-Koehler Publishers.

Lerner, M. (2000). *Spirit matters: Global healing and the wisdom of the soul.* Charlottesville, VA: Hampton Roads.

Neal, J. A.. (2008). Leadership and spirituality in the workplace. Retrieved from http://www.judineal.com/pages/pubs/leadership.htm. (Accessed on February 29, 2020).

Murchú, D. Ó. (1998). *Reclaiming spirituality: A new spiritual framework for today's world*. Spring Valley, NY: Crossroad Publishing.

Rehm, M. (1990). Vocation as personal calling: A question for education. *The Journal of Educational Thought (JET)/Revue de la Pensée Educative, 24*, 114–125.

Rimanoczy, I. B. (2010). Business leaders committing to and fostering sustainability initiatives (Doctoral dissertation). Teachers College, Columbia University.

Sinetar, M. (1987). *Do what you love. The money will follow*, Des Plaines, IL: Dell Pub.

Stephan, N. (1989). *Finding your life mission: How to unleash that creative power and live with intention*. Peterborough, NH: Stillpoint Publishing.

Tisdell, E. J. (2003). *Exploring spirituality and culture in adult and higher education*. Hoboken, NJ: John Wiley & Sons.

Tsao, F. C. & Laszlo, C. (2019). *Quantum leadership: New consciousness in business*. Palo Alto, CA: Stanford University Press.

Wong, P. T. (1998). *Implicit theories of meaningful life and the development of the personal meaning profile*. Mahwah, NJ: Lawrence Erlbaum Associates Publishers.

Zohar, D. & Marshall, I. (2000). *SQ: Connecting with our spiritual intelligence*. New York, NY: Bloomsbury Publishing.

12 Principle number 11

Oneness with Nature

Definition

Understanding that we are one with Nature, a species within species, is a powerful spiritual experience that can shape behaviors leading to a more harmonious relationship with each other and all beings.

Teaching Goal

Students have an experience in Nature.

Meta Goal

To understand that we are one with Nature, that we are a species within species, and that all Nature is within us.

Origins of the Principle

In a previous chapter, we signaled the relationship between humans and Nature in addressing the Principle *Interconnectedness*, a key to developing a systemic perspective. Now we continue in the content area of Spiritual Intelligence, and we will explore *Oneness with Nature* from a different angle: From the existential perspective.

My first thought of the role that Oneness with Nature has in a Sustainability Mindset originated when analyzing the interviews in my research. Several of the interviewed leaders shared experiences of their interactions with Nature that filled them with awe and had an impact on their thinking about their work and their environmental footprint. This led me to explore how we could intentionally develop such a sense of belonging *in and with* Nature, as opposed to the more anthropocentric understanding that Nature is *something that we need* or has to be cared for.

Environmentalist David Suzuki observed that over time we have cut ourselves off from the web of life; instead of seeing ourselves connected physically and spiritually to Nature, we live via the mind, as individuals separated from each other "on a lifeless, dumb world beyond the body" (Suzuki, 2007, p. 275). He reflects that attitudes about saving the environment need to be imbued again with a sense of sacredness.

Aboriginal people do not believe that they end at their fingertips but rather that their selves extend into the world around them. David Kinsley (1995, p. XV) commented on this extensively in his study about Ecology and Religion. He realized that the central questions of ecology, such as:

Are human beings primarily of Nature, or above, or apart from Nature?
Is our destiny to shape, perfect, develop, or accept the natural world and conform to it?

are, in fact, similar to theological questions:

What is our place or role in the creation?
Are we at home on the Earth or sojourners?
Where is our place in the order of hierarchy?.

The answers to these questions have important consequences in how we cohabit with each other and how we relate to our environment.

Aboriginal cultures across the world share a common understanding that their identity is linked to the land. Religious rituals surround their hunting of other species, emphasizing respect, and honor of the larger order to which both species belong. The Australian Aborigines, for example, consider that each person is related to specific animal and plant species, and their totemic identities signal common ancestors. Their relationship to their totem plant or animal is one of utmost respect, rather than manipulation for utilitarian ends. They are part of a symbiotic harmony, Kinsley notes. When we move from one location to another for work, education, or leisure, we transit through the land in a thoughtless manner, disconnected from it. In contrast, Aborigines understand they *are* the land (Kinsley, 1995, p. 31).

The *Stories about the Distant Time*, an oral history of the Alaskan and Yukon people, describes an age where animals were themselves human, demonstrating their kinship and providing a code of behaviors with the land and with other species (Kinsley, 1995, p. 38). This code included not being wasteful, not harvesting or killing any more than what will be used, and respectfully disposing what is unusable. Similar practices are found in other aboriginal cultures, like the Native American tribes or the Penan people in Sarawak, Malaysia. When the latter were trying to stop a government decision to relocate the group in order to make way for the construction of several dams, they explained that their ancestral home represented who they are—their identity—and that they weren't opposing the construction for the survival of their tribe, nor to defend the rainforest, but rather because they were all part of each other and the land. However, to better address the government, they "translated" this into a functional worldview and indicated that what was at stake was their "supermarket" and their "homes," not just a piece of land to be cleared.[1]

The indication to behave in an ethical way with the Earth is also present in Eastern religions. While for the Aborigines the connection to the land is related to subsistence of the human/environment system, in Eastern spiritual traditions it is about a sense of unity with all that is. Hinduism considers the universe as a living being, and one becomes a Hindu by learning the story of the land.

Rivers, fire, and wind are revered deities that will recipro-
cate the good treatment received. The Earth goddess, for
example, is offended by immoral, unethical, or criminal
activities (Kinsley, 1995, p. 58). The human organism is
seen as identical to the wider world; for example, in Tantric
yoga, the body is a miniature replica of the universe. This
monistic cosmovision contrasts with the dualistic worldview that permeates thinking and behaviors in the West,
where human beings are separate and distinct from Nature.

In Chinese traditions, the vital force (ch'i) is present
in all things (Wing-tsit, 1969). The cosmos is an organism tending toward harmony, with alternating forces of
growth and change. The complementarity is depicted in
the yin/yang, with the seeds of one present in the other.
Humans are meant to flow with this Principle, yielding
to change without resisting it (Kinsley, 1995, p. 72). This
law of harmony offers guidance to human behaviors and
is similar to the Taoist "effortless effort," folding oneself
into what is without trying to obstruct or manipulate it.
Recognizing the cycles of Nature and seeing humans as
an integral part of these resonates with the Principle of
Cyclical Flow, and as we have seen before, has positive
consequences on our sustainability behaviors.

This worldview is different from the Confucian view,
which reveres as sacred not the energy of the cosmos, but
rather the sacred energy found in human society. The
mission of humanity is to be good stewards, responsible
guardians of all creation (Kinsley, 1995, p. 78). From this
perspective, Christianity has also stated the responsibility
and superiority of humans to care for all species. Kinsley
describes a range of interpretations of the Bible, from
the anthropocentric extreme, with humans as rulers and
dominators of all Nature, through to the other extreme,
where humans are expected to show responsible stewardship of all species and the Planet. The Pope's Encyclical
Laudato Si (Francis, 2015) is an expression of the latter,
in an attempt to promote a much-needed sensitivity and

consciousness of the world's planetary challenges, and the role we can play.

The anthropocentric view was particularly reinforced by the Scientific Revolution, in the 16th through 18th centuries. The Enlightenment centered on mind-over-matter dualism, with Earth as an inanimate object of study to be explored, understood, and mastered. As occurs throughout history, the philosophical waves may be ridden just by a minority of the population, yet their influence in shaping the governing paradigms is paramount. The modern view that started almost four hundred years ago sees Homo sapiens at the top of the species pyramid, with unparalleled capacity to invent, create, and solve problems. We can see this paradigm pervading our contemporary global culture, if such a thing exists, through values (beliefs) including the superiority of our ego and our will, the priority given to satisfying our needs and desires, the instrumental utilization of natural resources, the ingenuity to invent, and the confidence that technology and human creativity have no limits. For example, we are convinced we will be able to figure out new solutions to global warming, and to everything else—not just here but anywhere in the universe—including Mars where we are talking about settling next!

From this anthropocentric perspective, Nature is an object to be analyzed and dissected, very different from the symbiotic human/land conceptions described previously. While individuals are not generally philosophers, paradigms pervade our world and our lives—and become visible through the behaviors resulting from the paradigm. Thus, with the best intentions, we participate in the manipulation of Nature by way of science and technology to serve our human needs and desires.

Before we fully realized the implications of this anthropocentric paradigm, Nature became a resource for our "progress." Theologian Douglas John Hall describes this progress as the evolution from Nature controlling human life to "a paradise in which humans control Nature by establishing a technocracy" (Hall, 1990, p. 82). Considering the great advances in human health, longevity, transportation, communications, agriculture, and technological connectivity, the experiment has been successful. Globalization has made the planet one big marketplace and low-cost production and fast shipping fills homes in urban areas with objects and food from across the world.

But the connectivity also brought us information, and we can now see images from around the globe on our phones. Weather-related events impact communities and regional economies, while governments are ill prepared to respond to disasters of many kinds. Industrial agriculture injects antibiotics into the food we consume and our immune system is altered. Plastics from our products flow into our waterways and oceans and become part of marine life. Overfishing and fertilizers create ocean dead zones. In a few weeks, COVID-19 changed the landscape and erased national borders, impacting not only world health, but also the entire global economy—and the people within it. Access to technology shows us the cost of our achievements and makes us realize its impact on our quality of life, not to mention a lack of purpose and meaning that is so frequently observed in our communities (Softas-Nall & Woody, 2017). Something has to change.

Why do we need this Principle?

Numerous recent studies have shown that the connection with Nature is not only important for our happiness but also leads to pro-environmental behaviors (Fretwell & Greig, 2019; Tsao & Laszlo, 2019, p. 141; Whitburn, Linklater, & Abrahamse, 2020). Studies have shown the connection between a sense of oneness with Nature and responsible consumer behaviors. Kunchamboo, Lee, & Brace-Govan (2017) observed that when the self-dilutes to become one with Nature, individuals develop a sense of mutual care as they progress from functional to spiritual attachment. The opposite is also true: Lack of connectedness with Nature leads to anxiety, depression, and disregard for environmental or social actions (Tsao & Laszlo, 2019, 141). This has been described as Nature Deficit Disorder, paraphrasing Attention Deficit Disorder (Louv, 2005).

The early reactions to the anthropocentric, dualistic worldview were found in the U.S. in the writings of several philosophers—each influenced by those who came before them—between the mid-1800s and 2000s: Ralph Waldo Emerson (1803–1882), his student Henry David Thoreau (1817–1862), John Muir (1838–1914), Aldo Leopold (1887–1948), and Thomas Berry (1914–2009). In the history of environmental ethics, their voices were alerting to similar concerns. Thoreau critiqued the scientific approach to Nature because it denied our communion with it and the spiritual nourishment it represents (Thoreau, cited by Worster, 1979, p. 87). Muir denounced that the human spirit was being choked by civilized life and lobbied for wilderness preservation (Muir cited by Nash, 1973, p. 127). Leopold called "resourcism" the tendency to see Nature only as a resource to meet human needs. In order to feel the oneness with the land, he invited "thinking like a mountain," which meant to have a long-term perspective and see the connections of all life forms. In 1988, eco-theologian Thomas Berry called for a new vision for human dignity, curbing the behaviors that were destroying the Earth. The technological wonderland is converting our planet into a wasteland, he posited, threatening human survival (Kinsley, 1995, p. 153, p. 173).

At this point, the reader will have noted the recurrent values of control, dominion, separation and fragmentation, autonomy and independence, and achievement and progress that the anthropocentric view of Nature elicits, and which are at the root of many of our planetary challenges. The experience of oneness with Nature (and all that is) can help us find our way back home, and educators can develop this.

How is this Principle effectively brought into the classroom?

This Principle is translated into the following Goals:
Teaching Goal:

Students have an experience in Nature.

Meta Goal:

To understand that we are one with Nature, that we are a species within species, and that all Nature is with us.

It is to be noted that the content area of Spiritual Intelligence, to which this Principle belongs, calls for *experiential* activities. While students in theological or environmental studies may intellectually explore theories and frameworks, the cognitive approach may not be the most appropriate for developing Spiritual Intelligence, and particularly the Principle of Oneness with Nature.

In most of the cases, students have profound experiences of oneness with Nature as a result of simple exercises, including as we will see below, simply spending one hour in Nature. Their experiences can even be transformative, leading them to reshape some of their values and behaviors.

These experiences in Nature can then be linked to how the anthropocentric paradigm has played, and still does play, a role in our culture, now with visible consequences. As students are institutionally "trained" to have intellectual activities, they will find the anthropocentric worldview a rich and complex content to ponder. They may feel more comfortable discussing the benefits and downsides of said paradigm and even recognize it at play in their own lives, which may lead to some habit changes. For this reason, the suggested sequence is to first assign an experiential activity and discuss the paradigm only afterward.

Key components

The key components in this Principle are as follows:

- *Experiential learning in Nature*;
- *Anthropocentric values related to this Principle and their consequences*; and
- *Exploration of the Self ⇔ Nature relationship.*

As indicated before, Spiritual Intelligence cannot be developed in a directly cognitive way. This Principle, although it has some intellectual components to it, is best approached through the path of an *experience*, which should be assigned first. Over and over, I have marveled at the power of simple exercises that invite students to have an experience in Nature. This has been particularly powerful when teaching in urban environments, but not exclusively. It highlights that students in higher education rarely, if ever, are given such an assignment. One of the simplest and more powerful exercises is spending one hour in Nature (See the full description of this exercise in *An Exercise to try out*). I have used this exercise with great success with students from different countries and regions of the world and in faculty development programs.

The instructions have gone through a series of revisions over time to improve the results. For example, there were some cases where students completed the assigned exercise but were not able to extract significant meaning from it. Their reflections were intellectual and based on theories or readings, but devoid of personal insights. In analyzing the cases, I realized that these individuals didn't invest the suggested amount of time, staying in the location for only a short time. Other individuals simply "imagined" that they were in Nature, without actually being so. In other cases, students combined their daily running activities with the exercise. In this situation, the assignment was folded into a familiar activity, which undermined the impact of the exercise since learning is enhanced in *unfamiliar* situations.

Regularly practiced sporting activities deprive the individual of the empty space that can prompt the oneness experience, since the focus becomes the routine or the physical performance of the sport. Another refinement to the instructions was to complete the exercise without their pets, because this is also a familiar activity, focusing the individual's attention on the animal's movements or its interactions with the environment. Merely stepping into the front- or backyard may also be excessively familiar and not provide the sufficient "estrangement stimulus" for a richer experience.

In the previous sections, we explored the role of the *anthropocentric paradigm* and the countless implications it has brought into our lives, for several centuries now. In Chapter 9, we addressed the values anchoring us in unsustainability, and in this Principle of Oneness, we have another opportunity to scrutinize some of these values. The anthropocentric paradigm is best introduced when connected to the particular discipline taught. How does it play in architectural design and concepts? How does it play in economics, biological science, politics, supply chain or hospitality management, strategy, design, farming, or in the arts? Independent of the subject that the educator is teaching, there will be multiple connections to the anthropocentric paradigm. This is no magic—it's simply the paradigm in which we are all living. So far.

Fortunately, more and more opportunities arise where educators are able to shine a light into the water in which we are all swimming, such that the paradigm becomes visible and alternatives can be considered. In this case, the discussion can include values such as control, human superiority, achievement and progress, globalization, autonomy and independence, comfort and wealth. The educator can complete the list of values with others that may be relevant to the discipline being taught or to the particular context. However, the conversation should start with the appreciated, recognized values of our paradigm before going into the unwanted implications.

This conversation on values can then be easily linked to the personal relevance of certain anthropocentric values for the student. Assignments fostering introspection and reflective essays about the *relationship of the student with Nature* and how certain values are more important for the individual than others are valuable pedagogical approaches to implement this Principle.

Preparing yourself for the task

Key questions for the educator:

For self-awareness:

- How do you relate to this Principle?
- Have you had an experience of oneness with Nature? If so, what did it mean, what was the impact for you?
- If not, how could you have one yourself?

To prepare the assignments/activities:

- What are the characteristics of the audience, in terms of religious/ethnic background? Some religions make individuals very aware of their place in the Universe and among all that is. Aboriginals also have a deep understanding of this Principle and may be a great resource in the classroom.
- What are the possibilities and constraints related to assigning an activity in Nature (weather, proximity, safety, and schedule)?
- What is the best timing to give the assignment?
- What are the anthropocentric values that are more present in the discipline you teach?
- How is Nature considered in the subject you teach? What are the challenges and the opportunities?

Tips for the educator:

- **Grading criteria** of the assignments related to this Principle need to be clarified—such as depth, time spent in the activity and in the reflection—since there is no right or wrong answer.
- Spiritual experiences cannot be mandated, and the best an educator can do is to prepare a **conducive setting**, including slowing down the pace even as instructions are given to transmit the importance of making space for the experience.
- While some students may already bring to the classroom a previous sense of oneness, others may develop it during the course, and others may just be getting started. Research indicates that a one-time experience may not have consequences in a person's life (Furness, 2018), so **reinforcing** the learning with diverse activities and dialogs to make meaning can be a good pedagogical idea.
- **Avoid merely cognitive activities**, such as those centered on facts and data, and always schedule these *after* an experiential activity related to this topic.
- A simple **check-in question** at the start of a class can be a prompt for this Principle. For example: *What was your experience of Nature this morning?* When students listen to each other's answers, it will expand their thinking. In one class, a student said, "Nothing, I live in an apartment" (equating the experience of Nature with the outdoors.) Another student challenged the first student: *Don't you have a window to see a tree? The sky?* The educator can further contribute asking: *What about the food? Or our own body, isn't that an experience of Nature?* (Note that this check-in question is not the same as the hour in Nature exercise described below—which requires seeking out unfamiliar locations. The goal here is to make students aware of the presence of Nature everywhere.)

- When conditions allow, invite students to go to a place free of light pollution and look at the **starry sky**. This is an activity that can also be organized as a group outing. Watching the immensity of the night sky resets the perspective of our size, importance, and place in the larger universe.

- **A sunrise/sunset experience** is another activity that in certain contexts may be accessible. I have been fascinated by the number of people living on the Atlantic coast in Florida who have never watched a sunrise. To organize a group outing makes it fun, but it's suggested that once arrived at the location, everyone goes or stays on their own to have a more intense personal experience. Follow the experience with reflective essays or a dialog.

- **Reflective essays and journaling** are useful techniques to prompt introspection and help students pause and explore this topic.

- **An imaginary conversation with an animal** is an easy and playful exercise. Students can select the animal of their choice and then write a conversation. The value of this exercise is in the student naturally speaking for the animal, which requires stepping into the animal's perspective, into "its paws or hooves." How would that animal think and feel? What would the animal describe about how humans are living? The playfulness of the exercise allows for the emergence of intuitive wisdom about Nature, how we should connect and behave, etc.

- Activities that feature the **time scale of evolution since the Big Bang** or the formation of Earth can also be impactful. There are several materials available (see *Other Resources* in this chapter), like The Cosmic Walk, where students walk along a spiral made with a rope on the floor and stones or small objects represent evolutionary milestones. A text accompanies the walk and relates what happened when (e.g., *Four and half billion years ago the sun blasted-off clouds of elements and spun the rest into our* *solar system, planets formed.* [Walk to the next milestone]. *Over the next half a billion years the Earth cooled and an atmosphere began to form around it).* This exercise provides a physical perspective of time scale and where we are in that scale. The 12–month scale is another activity. The 12 months represent the passage of time from the Big Bang, which happens the first second of January, up to the present. On this scale, the time elapsed since the beginning of the Industrial Revolution to today is covered by the last half second (yes, as in 0.5/60th of a minute) of the year! (Russell, 2000, p 47).

An exercise to try out

An hour in Nature

This is a very simple exercise that provides students with a prompt to have an experience in Nature. It has only some minor constraints, in highly dense urban environments where it may be challenging to find a park and in cases where weather conditions don't allow time to be spent outside.

Instructions:

> This exercise is about spending one hour in Nature. You can select the location, which should be a place that is not too familiar for you. For example, avoid your backyard. The less familiar, the better. Find a place to stand or sit. You can walk, but divide your time equally between sitting and walking. Go without your phone, any musical or electronic device, or a book or any reading or writing material. Go alone, don't take your pet with you. Don't take food with you. Don't combine the exercise with any sporting activity: No roller blading, skating, jogging, swimming, surfing, etc. The exercise is about just being with yourself in Nature, for one hour. Don't cut it short, although feel free to stay longer if you desire.

When you get back, write down your feelings, reflections, and insights from the experience in a reflective essay. This should be a personal essay about the experience, not a literature review or intellectual paper. It will be graded based on the depth of your reflections, your spontaneity, and the time invested in writing the essay.

A story

I was invited to teach a module about the Sustainability Mindset for management undergraduate students at the Universidad de Navarra, Spain. I gave them the assignment of one hour in Nature and I marveled at what occurred. For reasons that I still don't fully understand, many students spontaneously wrote in a very poetic way, some actually writing poems about their experience. The beauty and depth of those essays was such that I thought they should be published. I shared the idea of a book of student essays with my colleague Ekaterina Ivanova. The idea evolved and became a new book project—a book that would start with students' essays describing some transformational learning experience that challenged or impacted their mindset. Each essay would be followed by a section written by the writer's professor, detailing what exercise or contents prompted such a mindset shift. We prepared a Call for Contributions and in a few weeks we had twenty abstracts from Europe, North and South America, Asia, Oceania, and Africa, for what will be an inspiring testimony of a mindset shift taking place across the globe.

Other resources

The Cosmic Walk: Created in the mid-1980s by Sister Miriam Therese MacGillis, of Genesis Farm in Blairstown, New Jersey. She has inspired many adaptations. The most complete list of versions and resources to implement this activity can be found here. http://www.rainforestinfo.org.au/deep-eco/cosmic.htm#background

Movie: "The Planetary Collective –Overview" The 19-minute free trailer is a powerful video about the experience of the first astronauts that flew to the moon, and saw the planet from afar for the first time. https://vimeo.com/55073825

TED Talk by Mike deGruy, underwater filmmaker. *How I got hooked by an octopus.* https://www.ted.com/talks/mike_degruy_hooked_by_an_octopus

TED Talk by ocean researcher Sylvia Earle https://www.ted.com/talks/sylvia_earle_my_wish_protect_our_oceans

Book: *Ishmael* by Daniel Quinn: This 1992 philosophical novel gives the voice to a gorilla who has a conversation with a person. The novel examines the hidden cultural biases driving modern civilization and explores themes of ethics, sustainability, and global catastrophe.

Note

1. Personal communication, Bintulu. (2006). The Penan are part of the oldest inhabitants of the land, and together with other 17 ethnic groups constitute 11.8% of the Malaysian population. See The Borneo Project https://borneoproject.org/

References

Francis, P. (2015). *Laudato si: On care for our common home.* Huntington, IN: Our Sunday Visitor.

Fretwell, K. & Greig, A. (2019). Towards a better understanding of the relationship between individual's self-reported connection to nature, personal well-being, and environmental awareness. *Sustainability, 11*(5), 1386.

Furness, E. (2018). *Ecological restoration and connection to nature* (Doctoral dissertation). Cardiff University: Cardiff, UK

Hall, D. J. (1990). *The steward: A biblical symbol come of age* (Rev. ed.). Grand Rapids, MI: Eerdmans.

Kinsley, D. R. (1995). *Ecology and religion: Ecological spirituality in cross-cultural perspective.* London: Pearson College Division.

Kunchamboo, V., Lee, C. K., & Brace-Govan, J. (2017). Nature as extended-self: Sacred nature relationship and implications for responsible consumption behavior. *Journal of Business Research, 74,* 126–132.

Louv, R. (2005). *Last child in the woods: Saving our children from nature-deficit disorder.* Chapel Hill, NC: Algonquin.

Nash, R. (1973). *Wilderness and the American mind.* New Haven, CN: Yale University Press.

Russell, P. (2000). *The global brain awakens: Our next evolutionary leap.* Boston, MA: Element.

Softas-Nall, S. & Woody, W. D. (2017). The loss of human connection to nature: Revitalizing selfhood and meaning in life through the ideas of Rollo May. *Ecopsychology, 9*(4), 241–252.

Suzuki, D. (2007). *The sacred balance: Rediscovering our place in nature, updated and expanded.* Vancouver, BC, Canada: Greystone Books Ltd.

Tsao, F. C. & Laszlo, C. (2019). *Quantum leadership: New consciousness in business.* Palo Alto, CA: Stanford University Press.

Whitburn, J., Linklater, W., & Abrahamse, W. (2020). Meta-analysis of human connection to nature and proenvironmental behavior. *Conservation Biology, 34*(1), 180–193.

Wing-tsit, C. (1969). *A source book in Chinese philosophy.* Princeton, NJ: Princeton University Press.

Worster, D. (1979). *Nature's economy: The roots of ecology.* Oakland, CA: Sierra Club Books: Anchor P/Doubleday.

13 Principle number 12
Mindfulness

Definition

Mindfulness is being fully present, experiencing connectedness with all that is. Mindfulness enhances awareness and compassion and predisposes to social and environmental actions.

Teaching Goal

Students experience several different contemplative practices to have the opportunity to find what works best for them.

Meta Goal

To develop appreciation of the power of contemplative practices and develop new habits that increase mindfulness.

Origins of the Principle

One of the surprising observations in my research was that several business leaders mentioned they practiced some kind of mindfulness activity: Running, walking or sitting in the woods, meditating. They explained that this helped them get centered, something they felt was much needed given their daily leadership challenges.

Mindfulness is first mentioned in the Buddhist tradition, although it is independent of a particular belief system (Black, 2011). Yet, it has a spiritual condition. All the world's wisdom traditions declare that there is a realm of sacred meaning and knowledge that can be accessed through certain rituals (Elgin, 2010, p. 109), and mindfulness is one of those rituals. Both a process and a result, mindfulness has been associated with meditation, but there are many other contemplative practices that help develop mindfulness.

So what is mindfulness? It is an alert consciousness. The characteristic of mindfulness is a state or an experience of awareness of self, our emotions, and thoughts, in a noncognitive way. It is described as a direct-intuitive experience that creates a sense of wholeness, of connectedness with all that is (Tsao & Laszlo, 2019, p. 172).

Individuals find it challenging to describe their mindfulness experiences. This can be linked to the fact that it is actually a nonverbal experience, but also to the fact that we have not been taught how to talk about these experiences. We sense something, but we don't know how to put it into words. A busy, action-oriented colleague once reflected, "I realized I needed to do more being…," and we both laughed at her choice of words. We are more accustomed to engaging in actions, to making sense by reflecting, analyzing, and making logical statements—all valuable activities in the rational realm of knowing. However, the knowing that we tap into through a practice of mindfulness is different.

What the various contemplative practices have in common is that they create an alternative state of consciousness, where we are fully aware and present yet not concentrated on any particular line of thinking. It is a holistic experience characterized by its immediacy, which has also been recently made into a verb: *Presencing* (Scharmer, 2009; Senge, Scharmer, Jaworski, & Flowers, 2005). We can grasp this term in an intuitive way, since it is common for our minds to freely wander, jumping from the past to the future, from what just happened to what we will do later, giving relatively little attention to the present moment. To be fully present requires us to notice (but not dwell on) our thoughts, be aware of our body, and listen or observe intentionally. It is not an easy exercise and requires practice.

Economics professor Clair Brown from University of California, Berkeley, is a long-term meditation practitioner who brings mindfulness into her classroom. She describes it as an exercise "of being aware of the moment without judging, relaxing the body, quieting the mind, and opening the heart." In her Buddhist Economics seminar, students sit in silence for five to ten minutes and consider this one of the most profound lessons (Brown, 2017, xvi).

Neuroscientists have studied the impact that regular meditation has on the brain, observing structural and functional changes due to neuroplasticity. The benefits of mindfulness practices have also been noted in the health of individuals, reducing stress levels, and contributing to general well-being (Kabat-Zinn, 2005). In recent decades, meditation has also been introduced in progressive work-places, to help employees feel more balanced and happy. Satish Kumar, founder of the holistic Schumacher College, warns that being mindful doesn't automatically mean it is for good and suggests to ask: Is my mindfulness bringing benefit or harm? (Kumar, 2017, p. 53). For example, some studies have questioned the instrumental use of mindful-ness practices to manipulate the workforce into higher levels of productivity (Carrette & King, 2005, cited by Wamsler et al, 2018, p. 151).

That said, "harmful" or "manipulative" in association with mindfulness is uncommon and is not the aim that pioneering Chinese business leader and author Frederick Chavalit Tsao describes in his book, *Quantum Leadership: New Consciousness in Business*, coauthored with Case Western Reserve University professor Chris Laszlo. In Tsao's sections of the book—the two authors wrote separate chapters—he explains at length how he developed a holistic approach to leadership that encompasses not just himself, but all his organizations, and the employees and communities asso-ciated with them. For both authors, mindfulness practices operate under the principles of Quantum Physics, connect-ing the individual to a universal field of energy. This can take place, for example, in Nature or through music, artistic expressions, walking, journaling, practicing yoga, etc. These experiences augment the sense of interconnectedness and oneness with all that is, resulting in expanded levels of caring (Laszlo, 2020; Tsao & Laszlo, 2019). For example, short periods of meditation that focus on loving-kindness showed statistically significant effects on environmental mastery, purpose, mindfulness, and self-acceptance, among others (Fredrickson, Cohn, Coffey, Pek, & Finkel, 2008, cited in Tsao & Laszlo, 2019, p 141).

A thorough literature review on sustainability and mindfulness conducted at the Lund University Centre for Sustainability Studies indicated that between 2009 and 2014, the references to mindfulness in science-, art- and humanities-related papers increased by 30% per year (Ericson, Kjønstad, & Barstad, 2014, cited by Wamsler et al, 2018). The review identified the introduction of the concept of Ecological Mindfulness first in the 2000s (Mueller & Greenwood, 2015; Sol & Wals, 2015, cited by Wamsler et al, 2018), as well as the suggestion of a *Mindfulness Revolution* that develops awareness of the values and emotions contributing to unsustainable behaviors (Hanh, 2008; Kaza, 2008, cited by Wamsler et al, 2018, p. 148). Furthermore, mindfulness is found to develop compassion as opposed to fear, a very important and positive emotion required for the challenging times in which we are living (Ryan, 2016, p. 9). Other scholarly papers identified in the Lund literature review highlighted the impact of mindfulness on social actions, facilitating flexible behaviors, and innovation, as well as minimizing automatic responses—all important aspects of a sustainability mindset in action.

This connects with an empirical study that found a correlation between mindfulness and motivations toward "other-focused" behaviors, particularly climate action and pro-environment actions. Mindfulness appears to promote sustainable consumption behaviors, human ⇔ Nature connections, sensitivity to inequity, social activism, and activation of an individual's core values (Wamsler & Brink, 2018).

Which leads us to the next question.

Why do we need this Principle?

Part of my research included asking the interviewed individuals what advice they had for educators, and a few mentioned that mindfulness practices were something that didn't exist in their education; they believed it was important to spark awareness of mindfulness earlier in life.

Interestingly, the University of Lund expert in urban resilience and climate change adaptation, Professor Christine Wamsler, came to a similar conclusion. After years of researching and teaching about risk minimization and the development of sustainable cities, she began to think that something was lacking in the approach to sustainability education. An empirical study she conducted indicated that while there was a correlation between mindfulness and proenvironment behaviors, it was mainly focused on adaptation and resilience, rather than developing an anticipatory, preventative mindset (Wamsler & Brink, 2018). The more she delved, the more she found mentions of the need to address sustainability "from within," both in scientific research and in teaching. The International Panel for Climate Change, for example, recommended the need to address changes to behavior in order to accelerate social transformation (Kolstad et al, 2014; Stern et al, 2016). In 2014, the United Nations Framework Convention on Climate Change asked Buddhist leader Thich Nhat Hanh to provide a statement on climate change from his spiritual perspective, underscoring the realization that the inner dimension of the individual could play a significant role. Other religious and secular spiritual voices have published manifests and pledges, pointing to the spiritual dimensions of sustainability (see Interfaith statements in the *Resources* section of this chapter). Wamsler became an advocate for incorporating mindfulness practices into sustainability education, noting that there is a scarce and fragmented understanding of the internal dimensions of individual sustainable (and unsustainable) behaviors.

She is not alone with her concern. Human consciousness researcher Peter Russell stated it in these words: *"We ask what we can do about the world, rather than about ourselves"* (Russell, 2000, p. 114). The Academy of Management regularly clusters relevant topics into divisions and interests groups, yet it is the members and scholars themselves who are increasingly connecting the sustainability group (called Organizations and the Natural Environment) with the spirituality group (titled Management, Spirituality, and Religion). Texas A&M University Professor Louis (Jody) Fry saw in spiritual leadership a "being-centered" path to developing the concept of a "global mind" (Egel & Fry, 2017), with the understanding that in the journey from "me" to "we," we may experience the interconnectedness that could accelerate a new mindset (Scharmer, 2009).

The Indian concept of Darshan indicates that enlightenment is contagious (Russell, p. 150). This opens a gateway for educators to awaken in their students a sense of wholeness leading to sustainability actions. The next section addresses how.

How is this Principle effectively brought into the classroom?

This Principle is translated into the following Goals:
Teaching Goal:

Students experience several different contemplative practices to get the opportunity to find what works best for them.

Meta Goal:

To develop appreciation of the power of contemplative practices and develop new habits of practice that increase mindfulness

The reader may have noticed the progression through these 12 SM Principles, from the more concrete, information-based principle of Ecoliteracy, to the more intangible, intuitive, and deeper realms of self-development. This is not by chance. We are in the context of higher education or leadership development settings, and as such the suggested approach is to start with what feels more familiar and progressively journey into areas that are more personal, to which participants may be less accustomed. This allows for the creation of a trusting environment, which makes it safer to share thoughts and feelings with others.

This Principle, as with the previous one, calls for experiential activities. The teaching goal is to offer students the opportunity to experiment with a few contemplative practices, in the assumption that they may not be familiar with these types of experiences in the context of an educational institution. Some are quite simple, like observing a minute of silence or a few minutes of a guided meditation, and can be accommodated into nearly any context. To introduce them early in the course provides the chance to make these a small ritual to which students may grow accustomed, thus overcoming any initial reticence or discomfort with trying something new.

While the teaching goal is about exposure, the meta goal is to hopefully develop an appreciation of the "magic" power of these simple activities that have an impact well beyond the classroom.

Key components

The key components in this Principle are

- *Intuitive learning experience: Contemplative practices*
- *Intellectual learning experience: Discussion/Reflection connecting contemplative insights with values or habits*

The cornerstone of this Principle is undoubtedly the experience of different *contemplative practices*. There is no intellectual substitute for this. Tsao and Laszlo offer a detailed list of presencing practices, grouped into the following categories:

- Meditative practices from different spiritual traditions (prayer, Kabbalah, Sufi practices, transcendental, or other meditation, koans, shamanism) and of secular origin (i.e., workplace mindfulness practices, stress reduction mindfulness).
- Embodied practices that promote a mind-body-spirit integration through postures: yoga, Qigong, Tai Chi, martial arts, team sports, individual and competition sports, indoor and outdoor community activities.
- Practices in Nature, such as walking, being outdoors, forest bathing, gardening, etc.
- Artistic practices: music, art, dance, theater, painting, storytelling, writing, poetry.
- Rituals that celebrate a given place and time, e.g., harvest, water, soil, etc.

Presencing practices may be given as assignments or as voluntary activities, or a combination of both. They can be taken on as a group or in small groups; however, there should always be some individual activity. The debrief of the experience is a valuable component of the learning. It can be accomplished through a short dialog or exchange of impressions, or through written posts and reflective essays or journaling. To share the experience with peers is a particularly valuable step, especially at the beginning of the course when the novelty can make some participants anxious. Listening to their colleagues and seeing what they got out of it may inspire and encourage more timid students.

A simple way to incorporate some mindfulness practices is at the beginning of a class, as a check-in ritual. The activity sets a calm tone and breaks the perhaps frenzied rhythm with which students arrive at class. It can be a minute of silence, a short, guided meditation, or a minute of calming music.

In addition to offering the students different contemplative experiences to experiment, there are some *intellectual learning experiences* that can help develop mindfulness practices. After a debrief of some contemplative activity, the educator can link it with something that is relevant and connected to the discipline that is being taught or to previously covered or future topics. The most common connections might be with technology, speed, urban living, automatic versus thoughtful behaviors, self-scrutiny, lifestyle, values, and patience.

For example:

> *How does a silent time without doing anything connect with our habits of checking our phones, or being on the Internet?*
> *What is our relationship with technology; who is in charge? What may we be missing?*
> *What feelings did the student have while doing the activity? Anxiety? Peace? Impatience?*
> *How does this connect with our pace of life, and are we happy with that pace?*
> *What is the difference between a thoughtful presence and listening to someone versus rushed, multitasking, and superficial attention? What do we like best if we're on the receiving end?*
> *How is our pace when we are on vacation? In the countryside? What are we learning about ourselves, about our automatic behaviors, about our pace or lifestyle?*

Journaling and reflective essays are good complements to group dialogs and learning partners. They help go deeper, providing a structured space and time for otherwise neglected activities. Feedback has repeatedly indicated that these activities are more meaningful and important for their lives and relationships than the courses they are taking.

Preparing yourself for the task

Key questions for the educator:

For self-awareness:

- How do you feel about this Principle? Do you engage in any contemplative practices that bring you to a state of mindfulness? If not, which one could you start?
- What is the impact of a contemplative practice for your life?

To prepare the assignments/activities:

- Are there any students in the group who engage in some kind of contemplative practice? They can be a great ally and resource for inspiring others.
- What are some simple, brief rituals with which to start every class?
- What are the practices that could provide diverse experiences for your students?
- How can you connect mindfulness practices with the discipline you are teaching?

Tips for the educator:

- There are **four basic learning styles** in every group. The *What learners* are interested in theories and frameworks. The *Why learners* are interested in why something is important and why they should care. The *How learners* want to get into the task rapidly; they are eager to hear the instructions of what will happen. The *So What learners* are interested in what the activity will bring them personally, what benefit or use. To attend to different learning styles, introduce the exercises using the four questions: What will we do? Why is it important? How will we do it? So what? This introduction will not take more than one minute, yet it will increase the comfort and attention of the whole group (McCarthy & McCarthy, 2006).

This is particularly important with mindfulness practices: Students are not familiar with having this type of experience in an institutional context and, therefore, may be consciously or unconsciously anxious, reticent, or uncomfortable. Having a clear picture of what will happen helps everyone feel a bit more in control.

- Make the activities **voluntary**. While the preference is that everyone participates, there may be some students who are not ready for the activity (see Story below). However, invite the nonparticipating students to the debrief, because that may help them gain confidence and reassurance.

- Depending on the audience, **examples of others** in their same professional area can be inspirational and lower anxiety or feelings of inadequacy. I like to explain that mindfulness practices are offered in Executive Leadership programs and also in progressive workplaces, like Google or Nike. This has helped students reframe the activity and feel "privileged" to be participating in an exercise to which they otherwise would not have access.

- Seek to **foster new habits**: Invite students to select one mindfulness practice that they would like to continue. Learning partners can help for mutual support and encouragement.

- **Check-in rituals** create a different atmosphere, promoting thoughtfulness, being fully present, and connecting with feelings or personal insights. Questions are easy "check-in" techniques, for example:

  - What was the best of yesterday and why?
  - What was your experience of Nature this morning?
  - What brings you joy today?
  - What is one thing that you feel grateful for now?

It is important to give silent time—about one minute—to reflect. This way we create a space where everyone can get in touch with their own thoughts, since normally extroverts start talking immediately while the introverts don't get a chance to reflect (or if they do, they miss listening to their peers). A minute is neither too long nor too short to come up with an answer to this type of question.

* When the size of the group does not allow for everyone to share a check-in answer, or when the class schedule is tight and no more than a few minutes are available, the question can be asked, the silent minute respected, and then students can share with the person sitting next to them.

* The choice of the check-in questions is very important. Choose questions that foster insight and gratefulness. Avoid questions that are superficial (*What did you have for breakfast?*) or elicit negative feelings. You can contribute to a positive atmosphere of joy and lightness by selecting the appropriate questions. Remember, the energy is contagious.

* Another technique useful for check-ins or debriefs is called **Stop Reflect Write and Share**—a technique proposed by an introverted executive in a leadership development program. This simple process forces participants to write down their thoughts. There is always resistance to this as if we would be able to achieve the same result just thinking. But that is never the case. The pen always knows more than we imagine, and when we actually put pen to paper, different thoughts emerge. When we write, we follow a linear way of thinking, which is not the case when we think. *The Stop Reflect Write and Share* is also most powerful when using an actual piece of paper instead of typing into a cell phone or laptop because it is less familiar for

the students and pushes them out of their comfort zone. Unfamiliar circumstances offer the greatest learning opportunities.

An exercise to try out

Let the answer get to you

This exercise provides students with a simple prompt to connect with their intuitive, nonverbal knowing. It is done individually and can be done in 10–15 minutes once the person arrives at the selected location. It is recommended to debrief in the large group, so students hear how the experience was for others. Then the wrap up is about the opportunity to connect with our intuitive, nonverbal wisdom, how often we actually use that resource, why not, etc.

Instructions:

> This exercise is about having an experience with your own nonverbal, intuitive wisdom. Think of a current dilemma you are facing, something that you are concerned with. Write down the central question that best represents your challenge. Avoid yes/no questions.

Then go to some place in Nature. It doesn't have to be far away; just find a place where you can sit for 10–15 minutes, or walk. While you are there, look for the answer to your question. Pay attention because it is waiting for you and it will come to you in that short time. You just need to listen and observe very carefully, since you won't know where it will come from.

A story

This happened in a course I taught at Al Akhawayn University, Morocco, titled "Understanding self and the contemporary world", which covered the 12 Sustainability

Mindset Principles through personal reflections and an analysis of the planetary and regional challenges. We sat in a circle and as a way of doing our daily check in, I would bring a big vase to each session filled with wildflowers that I had picked on my way to class. The students were at first surprised and giggled, as they were not used to seeing an instructor do this, but then seemed to get used to it and stopped commenting after the second class.

Until one day, when the vase disappeared. When I arrived at the classroom, it was nowhere to be found. Interestingly, and without knowing what would await me, I had planned to start the day with an image I had seen on a TED Talk the night before. The image had three elements: a drawing of a mountain, the image of cell phones, and another drawing of a landfill, all in a horizontal linear sequence. It depicted how we take resources (rare minerals), convert them into objects soon to be disposed in a mountain of rubbish, only to replace them with new objects sourced from the earth. As the students were entering the classroom, I asked them to put their cellphones in the center of the room, in the place where the vase used to be. Each one of them asked, "Where is the vase?" in a concerned way that I didn't expect. I didn't think they noticed the vase after several days! I explained that it disappeared and they were very perturbed with the news.

We spent the first minutes in silence, looking at this changed centerpiece. Then they started to comment on the vivid experience, of how "Nature" (the vase with flowers) had been replaced by disposable objects.

During the break, some students approached me to find out more about the missing vase and some offered to buy a vase to replace the missing one.

The vase ultimately reappeared—it had been removed by the cleaning staff and placed elsewhere. When it returned, the students cheered, and we continued our meditation check-ins every subsequent class with flowers as the centerpiece.

At the end of the course, as we were taking group pictures, a student asked if she could bring and hold the vase for the picture.[1] This had become a meaningful symbol for their awareness journey.

Note

1. https://isabelrimanoczy.net/?page_id=1550

Other resources

Tree of Contemplative Practices. https://bhavanacreativity.word press.com/2018/09/24/tree-of-contemplative-practices/

https://www.arrcc.org.au/reflect-statements-by-faith-leaders includes Climate action kit for different religions: Buddhist, Christian, Hindu, Islamic and Jewish.

Meditation books for beginners:

Wherever You Go, There You Are by Jon Kabat-Zinn.

The Miracle of Mindfulness by Thich Nhat Hanh.

Mindfulness: An eight-week plan for finding peace in a frantic world by Mark Williams and Danny Penman.

Book *The Power of Now*—by Eckhart Tolle.

Video about The Power of Now—The 10 ideas. https://youtu .be/3_l-EovGdnA (29 min)

TED Talk about Meditation: Neuroscientist Amishi Jha talks about how to tame your wandering mind. https://www.ted.com/talks/ amishi_jha_how_to_tame_your_wandering_mind

TED Talk about the Right Brain hemisphere and nonverbal knowledge: Brain researcher Jill Bolte talks about how she studied her own stroke and what she learned about her recovery experiencing the world through her right brain hemisphere. https://www.ted .com/talks/jill_bolte_taylor_my_stroke_of_insight

TED Talk about the practice of stillness by Pico Iyer. https://www .ted.com/talks/pico_iyer_the_art_of_stillness?referrer=playlist-talks_to_help_practice_patienc

TED Talk about speed, by Journalist Carl Honore who believes the Western world's emphasis on speed erodes health, productivity, and quality of life. https://www.ted.com/talks/carl_honore_in_praise_ of_slowness?referrer=playlist-talks_to_help_practice_patienc

TED Talk about happiness by Matthieu Ricard, a biochemist turned Buddhist monk who talks about how to train our mind for serenity and well being. https://www.ted.com/talks/matthieu_ricard_the_habits_of_happiness?referrer=playlist-talks_to_help_practice_patienc
TED Talk by mindfulness expert Andy Puddicombe describes the transformative power of doing nothing. https://www.ted.com/talks/andy_puddicombe_all_it_takes_is_10_mindful_minutes?referrer=playlist-talks_to_help_practice_patienc

References

Black, D.S. (2011). A brief definition of mindfulness. Mindfulness Research Guide. Retrieved from http://citeseerx.ist.psu.edu/viewdoc/download?doi=10.1.1.362.6829&rep=rep1&type=pdf
Brown, C. (2017). *Buddhist economics: An enlightened approach to the dismal science*. NY, New York: Bloomsbury Publishing USA.
Carrette, J. & King, R. (2005). *Selling spirituality: The silent takeover of religion*. London: Routledge.
Egel, E. & Fry, L. W. (2017). Cultivating a global mindset through "being-centered" leadership. In J. Neal (Ed.), *Handbook of personal and organizational transformation*. Manhattan, NY: Springer International Publishing.
Elgin, D. (2010). *The living universe: Where are we? Who are we? Where are we going?* San Francisco, CA: Berrett Koehler Publishers.
Ericson, T., Kjønstad, B. G., & Barstad, A. (2014). Mindfulness and sustainability. *Ecological Economics, 104*, 73–79.
Fredrickson, B., Cohn, M.A., Coffey, K.A., Pek, J., & Finkel, S.M. (2008). Open hearts build lives: Positive emotions, induced through loving-kindness meditation, build consequential personal resources. *Journal of Personality and Social Psychology, 95*, 1045–1062.
Hanh, T. N. (2008). *The world we have: A Buddhist approach to peace and ecology*. Berkeley, CA: Parallax Press.
Kabat-Zinn, J. (2005). *Coming to our senses: Healing ourselves and the world through mindfulness*. London, UK: Hachette.
Kaza, S. (2008) *Mindfully green*. Boulder, CO: Shambhala Publications.
Kolstad, C., Urama, K., Broome, J., Bruvoll, A., Cariño Olvera, M., Fullerton, D., … & Mundaca, L. (2014). Social, economic and ethical concepts and methods. In: Edenhofer, O., Pichs-Madruga, R., Sokona, Y., Farahani, E., Kadner, S., Seyboth, K., & Minx,

J. C. (Eds.). *Climate change 2014: Mitigation of climate change. Contribution of working group III to the Fifth assessment report of the intergovernmental panel on climate change*, (pp. 173–248). Cambridge, UK: Cambridge University Press.

Kumar, S. (2017). *Soil, soul, society: A new trinity for our time*. Brighton, UK: Leaping Hare Press.

Laszlo, C. (2020). Quantum management: The practices and science of flourishing enterprise. *Journal of Management, Spirituality & Religion, 17*, 301–315. doi: 10.1080/14766086.2020.1734063.

McCarthy, B., & McCarthy, D. (2006). *Teaching around the 4MAT® cycle: Designing instruction for diverse learners with diverse learning styles*. Thousand Oaks, CA: Corwin Press.

Mueller, M. P. & Greenwood, D. A. (2015). Ecological mindfulness and cross-hybrid learning: A special issue. *Cultural Studies of Science Education. 10*, 1–4.

Russell, P. (2000). *The global brain awakens: Our next evolutionary leap*. Boston, MA: Element.

Ryan, K. (2016). Incorporating emotional geography into climate change research: A case study in Londonderry, Vermont, USA. *Emotion, Space and Society, 19*, 5–12.

Scharmer, C. O. (2009). *Theory U: Learning from the future as it emerges*. San Francisco, CA: Berrett-Koehler Publishers.

Senge, P. M., Scharmer, C. O., Jaworski, J., & Flowers, B. S. (2005). *Presence: An exploration of profound change in people, organizations, and society*. NY, New York: Crown Business.

Sol J. & Wals A. E. (2015). Strengthening ecological mindfulness through hybrid learning in vital coalitions. *Cultural Studies of Science Education. 10*(1), 203–214

Stern, P. C., Janda, K. B., Brown, M. A., Steg, L., Vine, E. L., & Lutzenhiser, L. (2016). Opportunities and insights for reducing fossil fuel consumption by households and organizations. *Nature Energy, 1*(5), 1–6.

Tsao, F. C. & Laszlo, C. (2019). *Quantum leadership: New consciousness in business*. Stanford, CA: Stanford University Press.

Wamsler, C. & Brink, E. (2018). Mindsets for sustainability: Exploring the link between mindfulness and sustainable climate adaptation. *Ecological economics, 151*, 55–61.

Wamsler, C., Brossmann, J., Hendersson, H., Kristjansdottir, R., McDonald, C., & Scarampi, P. (2018). Mindfulness in sustainability science, practice, and teaching. *Sustainability Science, 13*(1), 143–162.

Part VI

Weaving it all together

As we have transited through these different Principles, the reader will have noticed that they are inextricably linked. Like a scaffolding structure that allows educators to build their course contents with the assurance provided by a solid framework, each component of the structure is connected to several other parts.

For example, *Ecoliteracy,* clearly defined in this framework with its teaching goals and key components, can be seen as related to the Principle *My Contribution*, all the Systems Perspective Principles, *Creative Innovation* and *Reflection*, and *Oneness with Nature*. Less so with *Purpose* or *Self-Awareness*, yet that could probably be disputed. See Figure VI.1 for a map of the most obvious linkages among the Principles.

Educators may find their own best sequence in covering the Principles or let them emerge organically in their courses. Since they are meta-contents, designed to develop thinking habits rather than delivering information, I recommend naming them so students become aware of them as new thinking habits essential to a Sustainability Mindset. For example, in my courses, I introduce them briefly in the beginning and place a chart with the Principles' names and icons clearly visible in the classroom, which helps the students and me to make quick references at different times during the course. Sometimes when discussing a particular

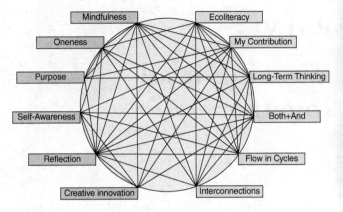

Figure VI.1 Interconnections among the SM Principles

topic, I invite students to point out what Principles are being or should be taken into account. For instance, when discussing 5G technology, they may look at the chart and say, "Who is thinking of the long-term impacts of 5G? Will it increase the information gap? And Interconnections! Have the health impacts been sufficiently tested?" This type of repeated referencing to the Principles helps embed the Principles as a new lens for analyzing facts, which is ultimately the goal.

Educators may also scan the Principles and check those that are already covered indirectly in their course contents. In such cases, they just have to be named, which develops intentionality in the new habit of mind. When the time constraints don't allow inclusion of all the Principles, I suggest choosing those that will have a greater impact given the discipline that is being taught. They can also be introduced all at once, with the students identifying those they need to develop more personally.[1] If a choice has to be made by the educator, those that should *not be left out* are *My Contribution, Reflection, Self-awareness, Purpose, and Mindfulness*. Understanding our own contribution is empowering and leads to actions, converting the weight of blame into the power of agency. Reflection is connected to all the other Principles and is a precious habit of mind to instill in the students because it permits them to pause during today's often frenzied pace and deepen their self-awareness. Self-awareness relates closely to the values that anchor us personally in unsustainability. It is a valuable gift we can offer the audience and becomes a powerful leverage for transformation. Something similar happens when we ask students about their Purpose, a question that is seldom if ever asked in higher education. This I believe is a missed opportunity, because addressing Purpose offers students a gateway for more peaceful and fulfilling lives, the same as exposing them to Mindfulness practices.

The interconnections between the Principles indicate that a mindset for sustainability is multilayered. It is the complex lens resulting from various intellectual processes for analyzing and regrouping information and is accompanied by profound personal insights. It spans the spectrum from the more concrete, cognitive facts to the most intangible and intuitive understanding.

This complexity is probably the reason why educators tend to shy away from working toward developing a sustainability mindset. They feel unsure of what it takes to develop such a mindset and may wonder if discussing values and beliefs could be considered intrusive and inappropriate in the context of an educational institution. In addition, it is an unfamiliar domain for the instructor herself.

For these reasons, I have attempted to address the complexity of the Sustainability Mindset presented in this book by breaking it into Principles and to present it to the educator with some easy ways to embed the main elements of the Mindset into their teaching. The Principles are general statements; they are not content-specific to any particular discipline. They constitute leverage points to develop a "way of thinking and being," as described in the definition in Chapter 1. Therefore, finding the intersections between the more general Principles and the particular discipline is essential. Questions such as *"How does both+and thinking connect with the subject you are teaching? How does the short-term thinking impact the discipline of your course?"* constitute prompts for the educator to tailor the Principles to a particular context.

A different pedagogy for new contents

In the beginning of this book, I signaled that a mindset for sustainability corresponds to an internal dimension, different from the external aspects educators teach in sustainability-related disciplines. This particularity calls for a different pedagogical approach and invites educators to play the role of a "learning facilitator," at least during some parts of their classes. Stepping out of the more traditional teaching role may be comfortable for some educators, but something infrequent, or even new, for others.

At the same time, the characteristics of today's student audience are in no way similar to students of a decade or two ago. The world is also no longer the same; the challenges and the awareness of these challenges have both increased, and the COVID-19 pandemic has brought every person on this planet an experiential lesson of global interdependency. Technology has shaped a new landscape and agendas such as the UN Sustainable Development Goals have laid out a roadmap for what we collectively need to aim at if we want to shape a world that works for all. Or if we want to stop shaping a world that is not working.

This is a different world, and our task as educators to prepare our students to thrive in this new world involves the new knowledge, competencies, skills, and attitudes they need. How we plan and implement that preparation is also a key to our students' success.

Pioneering voices have long called for new pedagogical approaches. Plymouth University Professor Stephen Sterling stressed as early as the 1990s the need for a new way of teaching—plus new content to address the sustainability challenges, including critical and systems thinking. He suggested that sustainability cannot be an "add-on"; instead, he posited, it required a change in our educational thinking and practice, for example, through deep learning, meaning a holistic, potentially transformative experience (Sterling 2004, p. 50). Canadian educator Ed Sullivan offered a transformative learning vision for the 21st century, focusing on the sustainability factor. He invited educators to "kindle the fire of the soul" and to educate with the human spirit in mind (O'Sullivan, 1999). We are educating *about* responsibility when we should be educating *for* responsibility, and this requires integrating emotions, insights, observation, and action within a *whole person learning method*, suggested New Zealand educator Ross McDonald (2013). Riane Eisler (2000) proposed a new way of education, based on partnership as opposed to the hierarchical domination model. A group of scholars stated in 2013 the educators' challenge: *How can we nurture students to be leaders in a sustainability revolution?* In response, they proposed teaching sustainability from the perspective of humanities and social sciences, which meant problem-based, project-based interdisciplinary learning, combined with liberal arts and reflective practices (Petersen Boring, 2013, p xiv). Along similar lines, a think tank about how business schools could serve people and planet called for new teacher competencies, such as coaching, mentoring, transdisciplinary collaboration, and a more holistic approach (Muff et al, 2013, p, 118). Increasingly, the need to revisit our pedagogical methods has been encouraged by experts in many fields, and indeed, it is one of the United Nations Principles for Responsible Management Education.

Wearing a learning facilitator or a coach hat may be less difficult than it sounds. "We have to put deep learning into the operating system of management education," writes David Cooperrider in the Foreword to the book

Stop Teaching (Rimanoczy, 2016, p. xiii). Deep, holistic learning will not only benefit future managers but students of any discipline. The urgency of developing students as agents of change is clearly understood by the Universities Global Coalition of University Presidents, a recent initiative of the UN Institute for Training and Research. Members realize that "universities not only have an opportunity, but an obligation, to do whatever is in their power to educate and inspire students to play an active role in addressing the most pressing issues confronting our world today, produce new ideas that can lead to new solutions and collaborate with other organizations to create awareness, support, and even lead local and global efforts."[2] Inspiration and engagement cannot be achieved with siloed contents and intellectual learning only. Educators can open new pedagogical pathways by asking themselves the following questions:

- How can I make my contents relevant to the students?
- What is the tacit knowledge that may be in the room, and how can I help bring it out?
- What are some appropriate ways to promote social learning, both from and with each other?
- What are some activities that can foster the key habit of reflection with the students?
- How can I create unfamiliar environments that will challenge them to shift their paradigm?
- How can I create an appreciative, positive atmosphere in the classroom?
- What can I do to address the full person and not just appeal to the student's mind?
- How can I help students take action?

We can do this

If philosophers shaped our tacit paradigm, the paradigm that doesn't seem effective any longer, who are the people who are today creating new narratives to envision and shape a better world in this planetary experiment?

Duane Elgin (2009) reflects that Nature evolves through cycles of growth, overgrowth, and ultimately balance through a decline. If we pay careful attention, we may notice that we are experiencing the consequences of overgrowth and the balancing act as they are happening—not in one stroke, but in several, diverse events. The Coronavirus, for example, spreads because we live in a globalized world with continuous interaction of people and goods. In a matter of few weeks, we discovered how interdependent we are. We realized how challenging it is to stay at home with our kids, which tests creativity and patience, but which also affords us the opportunity to have meaningful conversations and interactions with our family, something our "life as usual" didn't allow us. We are taking uncomfortable decisions, such as staying in self-quarantine because we don't want to put others, strangers included, at risk. Unexpectedly, we are expanding our scope of care. This is happening in our homes, within the limits of our cities or the borders of our nations, such as Italy, the first country to close its borders and self-quarantine 60 million inhabitants.

The history of humanity, Elgin posits, shows a movement of separation from Nature and others. It seems to me that we have started the journey toward a rediscovery of our connections.

As mentioned briefly in the Introduction of this book, a tide of new narratives is covering our planet. They articulate new moral codes, denounce the values that have hurt us, and offer healing and a path back to our hearts. The narratives emanate from a wide range of thought leaders, activists, and concerned community members who are witnessing the human development in front of their eyes. They include religious and secular spiritual leaders, economists, environmental activists, humanists, quantum physicists and social researchers, integral philosophers, and behavioral scientists. The diversity of those involved is striking. There are a growing number of circles of women (e.g., a movement called The Millionth circle) that have different contexts and aims, but are mostly focused on self-empowerment, entrepreneurship, mindfulness, and mutual support. Teenagers are involved with movements such as Extinction Rebellion. And inspired by Greta Thunberg, children of all ages are also finding ways to contribute their own new narratives.

And the list goes on! Journalists, writers, and poets. Grassroots leaders and movements. Think tanks, networks, and community circles. Aboriginals and social philosophers. Bloggers, filmmakers, and musicians. Artists and yes: educators.

All of these individuals and groups see themselves as outliers, which is natural since change never starts as mainstream. As Margaret Mead famously admonished, *"Never doubt that a small group of thoughtful, committed citizens can change the world; indeed, it's the only thing that ever has."* They find their own *"sangha,"* the community of like-minded others who help and encourage each other along the way. Some of these groups interact, some work in parallel universes with a kindred aim. They inspire each other and nurture their passion through seeing other change-makers, even if they never meet. They are creating much-needed healing zones because more unfamiliar territory is ahead of us.

Some years ago, I was wondering if I would live to see the famous evolutionary tipping point, where a critical mass of individuals would help redefine the new ways of living together on this blue planet. I no longer harbor doubts about witnessing this tipping point because we are already in the midst of it. I can see the journey of Campbell's hero, the trans-historical myth, at play again, at a collective level. We realize we have estranged from Nature and from each other in the pursuit of exploring the unknown. We have challenged our human limits, adventurous and fascinated with our big Self, our ego, the brilliant superiority of human species. We faced challenges, won some victories, but also fell into an abyss of despair, depression, anxiety, unhappiness, and disenchantment. This is part of the hero's journey and also the moment of revelation. It is the tipping point of transformation. Losing the ego, we find each other and ourselves. We return, changed, or as T. S. Eliot put it, that "the end of all our exploring will be to arrive where we started and know the place for the first time."

I see educators in a privileged position. They are not teaching students, they are developing change accelerators. Marine biologist pioneer Sylvia Earle dreams of creating *hope spots* in the ocean. I see educators today creating the hope spots of a civilization reunited with its soul.

Notes

1. This can also be done through the Sustainability Mindset Indicator, an automatic questionnaire to map and profile where an individual is on their personal journey toward a mindset for sustainability (in development, forthcoming 2021)
2. https://universityglobalcoalition.org/about/

References

Eisler, R. (2000). *Tomorrow's children: A blueprint for partnership education in the twenty-first century*. Boulder, CO: Westview Press.

Elgin, D. (2009). *The living universe: Where are we? Who are we? Where are we going?* San Francisco, CA: Berrett Koehler Publishing.

McDonald, R. (2013). *A practical guide to educating for responsibility in management and business*. New York, NY: Business Expert Press.

Muff, K., Dyllick, T., Drewell, M., North, J., Shrivastava, P., & Haertle, J. (2013). *Management education for the world: A vision for business schools serving people and the planet*. Cheltenham, UK: Edward Elgar Publishing.

O'Sullivan, E. (1999). *Transformative learning. Educational vision for the 21st century*. Toronto: Zed.

Petersen Boring, W. (2013). Introduction. In: Petersen Boring W. & Forbes W. (Eds.). *Teaching Sustainability: Perspectives from the humanities and social sciences.* (p. xv) Nacogdoches, TX: Stephen F. Austin State University Press.

Principles for Responsible Management Education. Retrieved from www.unprme.org

Rimanoczy, I. (2016). *Stop teaching: Principles and practices for responsible management education.* New York, NY: Business Expert Press.

Sterling, S. (2004). Higher education, sustainability, and the role of systemic learning. In: Corcoran P. B. & Wals A. E. J. (Eds.). *Higher education and the challenge of sustainability.* Dordrecht, The Netherlands: Springer.

Index

224   *Index*

CPSIA information can be obtained
at www.ICGtesting.com
Printed in the USA
BVHW042145270821
615503BV00013B/298